Alcibiades

Fact, Fiction, Farce

Jack Meyer

Order this book online at www.trafford.com
or email orders@trafford.com

Most Trafford titles are also available at major online book retailers.

Print information available on the last page.

ISBN: 978-1-4269-1833-9 (sc)
ISBN: 978-1-4269-1834-6 (hc)
ISBN: 978-1-4669-2397-3 (e)

Library of Congress Control Number: 2009936635

Trafford rev. 11/20/2023

Trafford
PUBLISHING   www.trafford.com

North America & international
toll-free: 844-688-6899 (USA & Canada)
fax: 812 355 4082

Also by Jack Meyer

The Odyssey of the Western Spirit: From Scarcity to Abundance 2nd Edition

Alcibiades: A Play in Three Acts

Special Thanks

Donn Pelegrin, Fred Kersten, Caroline Dumont, Pam Harris, Matt Van Sistine, Richard Golen, Jean Orsi, and Bob and Tina Meyer

A Note to the Reader

Quite obviously, Thucydides' account of the Peloponnesian War is one of the great treasures of the Western literary tradition. It stands at the pinnacle of excellence along with the *Dialogues* of Plato, the *Meditations* of Descartes, *The Critique of Pure Reason* of Kant, and *The Phenomenology of Spirit* of Hegel. These are works of clear genius that have come to constitute the rich tradition that is the Western Spirit. Thucydides is the main source for materials regarding the life of Alcibiades as he figures significantly in the War. The *Lives* of Plutarch include a sketch of the man that is eminently useful for his personal life. Passages in Plato, while limited in scope, provide additional accounts of the man's activities. On the basis of these facts, the life of Alcibiades is reconstructed which in turn leads into elements of fiction and farce. Fundamentally, the intent is to use the Greek experience as an analogue for a critique of American foreign policy. Fiction and farce facilitate this comparison. A plausible historical Alcibiades serves as a caricature for a discussion that has nothing to do with him. Along the way, the figure of Socrates serves as a voice of reason and judgment that carries the discussion into concerns of philosophical merit. His own hypothetical defense in his trial brings together the various aspects of political and military failure that may give us pause to reflect upon our own times.

☆ ☆ ☆

Being the son of Thucydides the Historian, I am named Thucydides the Younger. While my father rightfully stands in the light of historical genius, I myself work in the shadows, in the gray area between history and philosophy that is the privilege of hindsight. He was an active participant and enlightened chronicler of the great events surrounding the long war between Sparta and Athens, while I was a non-participant and simply had the advantage of living long after the war was decided with the demise of the Athenian Empire. A close friend of mine was Plato and he had that same advantage of longevity and we together discussed in depth this calamity to our beloved city. These discussions returned again and again to the stunning career of Alcibiades, a man of singular talent and daring audacity. Ward of Pericles, favorite student of Socrates, incredibly handsome and rich, brilliant tactical commander, rogue and scoundrel, and consummate traitor, this Alcibiades was the single person most responsible for the defeat of Athens. The city's own favorite son, this product of the Golden Age, was a man as morally corrupt as he was convincingly eloquent. He could get his way as the people easily deferred to his opinion. His story is worth recounting in detail as a point of departure for the far more important account of the greater events surrounding the Golden Age of Greece and its end.

In telling the story of my fellow Greeks it is possible to imagine a far greater reality. The Athenian Empire had the natural tendency to expand, to bring more and more area under its jurisdiction and control, as would any Empire. The absolute limit case of such an imaginary expansion would be if a single political and military entity were to dominate the entire world, if the globe itself were to be brought to heel under one central superpower. Such a reality is perhaps inconceivable but it is still possible so, in telling the story of Athens and its downfall, a story in small letters, as it were, it may be possible to consider the future of a global power, a possibility in large letters, and thereby make sense of the nature of empire itself. As a historian it is possible to consider the big and the small and then come to some sort of comparative philosophical conclusion regarding a central lesson of history. All of this requires a certain level of intellectual patience as history itself expounds an understanding that we may or may not heed. Not being a work of true scholarship, something that would adhere to a strict interpretation of the facts, the telling of this story is simply a focused reflection upon perennial issues of history and philosophy.

The issue is war, the war between Sparta and Athens that will conclude in disaster after 27 years of struggle. The dispersion of the Athenian Empire will leave a great legacy. It had been many years since the great allied victory over the Persians, when a slave army of the East met the citizen forces of the West and was defeated finally in the Straits of Salamis. Combined Greek forces marshaled by Athenian and Spartan leadership fought against overwhelming numbers and yet were decisively victorious. The Persians fled back to the East and the joyous Greeks settled into their Mediterranean homeland and resumed the building of a civilization like no other. But feelings and assurances of consensus were quickly tested as the unity split into two, that persistent bifurcation of human nature that usually ends in carnage. As the foreign enemy receded into a more distant memory, the Greeks moved toward disagreement and jealousy among themselves and nurtured enemies within. The wartime consensus was shattered upon the rocks of splintered partisan agenda. Athens built a naval alliance of common interest that was gradually and perhaps inevitably transformed into an Empire of central dominion. Allies were consulted less and less as their annual payments to the first city skyrocketed. The cost of Empire was great and everyone must be called upon to pay. The Athenians naturally came to be resented more and more. But there were advantages too. The Athenian Empire was an economic and cultural superpower. Innovation, initiative, expansion, and profit gravitated to the center. Power on this scale would necessarily impact everyone, everywhere, everytime, good, bad, or ugly. Perhaps Athens and Sparta were fated to come to blows as a gloriously shared past could not prevent a division that would encompass a ruthless slaughter. Sooner or later it would come, with the best bets on the sooner. The conflict that was on the horizon between these two, to be called the Peloponnesian War, would be a total war of violence and attrition, a fight to the finish. It would severely disrupt the Athenian miracle of democracy as forces of conservatism sought to prevail. But, in the name of all the gods of our antiquity, it was a battle of our own heartbreaking choosing. History, as my father believed, is about big events but it is nonetheless true that a single individual, Alcibiades, had very much to do with the eventual reduction of Athens.

☆ ☆ ☆ ☆ ☆

The sky is a deep clear blue and the market of Athens is bustling with vendors of all sorts unmercifully hawking their goods. Slaves and freemen, merchants and traders, people from everywhere, engage one another in a mingled chaos of everyday life in the capital city. In an area off to the side a group of young men are gathered around an older man, engaged in dynamic conversation. But attention is directed elsewhere as a group of boys are playing knucklebone in the road. They are in the way. A man from the country, burly and disheveled, is leading a horse drawn cart loaded with manure. He looks mean and nasty and is without humor. "Get out of the way you little varmints, commerce is coming through," he yells. The boys leap out of the way except for the one who will be identified as Alcibiades. He stands directly in front of the approaching cart and gives not an inch. Standing arms akimbo he glares at the man.

Alcibiades barks back in his cute sort of way. "This is our game and our place. Go some other way. Country bumpkins must stand aside before the new kids of the city. We are the youth and future of Athenian greatness." The man glares back in disgust but, refusing conflict, he reluctantly pulls to the side and bypasses the knucklebone game. Alcibiades stands proudly as his friends congratulate him on his audacity, or one might say, bodacity. Adult witnesses point to the boy. A bystander is heard to say. "That little troublemaker has attitude. He's a bad example to those other kids and he ought to be punished. A good beating would do that bad boy good."

"No," someone else say, "it shows spunk, something that our effeminate youth of today need more of. I bet one day that that little hellion will do something great."

A third witness says, "maybe something great, but more likely something devious and disastrous. Isn't that kid the ward of Pericles? Perhaps our great leader can make something out of him. He sure is good looking."

The boys gather about Alcibiades, all atwitter about his deed. He gives a little shove to one of the boys who resents the gesture and pushes back much harder. They tumble about in the dirt, the fight quickly escalating out of hand. Alcibiades is getting the worst of it so he resorts to biting the boy's arm. The boy screams and they leap apart and the wounded boy shouts.

"Alcibiades you fight like a girl!"

Alcibiades barks back. "No, I fight like a lion!" A dispersing crowd chuckles at the exchange, some impressed but most unsure, and none doubting the audacity of the good looking Alcibiades.

☆ ☆ ☆ ☆ ☆

A most unusual dinner party is being held at the home of Pericles. It is a small gathering that includes a rather large perspective. The playwright Sophocles is a close friend of Pericles and, as always, is working on a new play. Socrates is already a character in Athens and Pericles finds him to be useful. Aspasia, Pericles' companion, is a courtesan from Miletus whose beauty is surpassed only by her natural intelligence. She has recently made the acquaintance of the prophetess Diotima of Mantinea whose conversation is as engaging as it is mystifying. And, finally, there is the teenager Alcibiades who is deemed old enough to sit at the main table yet young enough hopefully to keep quiet.

The meal has been concluded, the dishes removed, and glasses refreshed with a splash of wine. Alcibiades remains at the table but is fidgeting enough to be both charming and annoying. Pericles speaks to Sophocles.

"Well, old friend, times are certainly good and matters of the empire always keep things active. Damn those Spartans! Do you find enough material for your play writing?"

Sophocles replies, "there's always enough material and I have yet to look beyond our city limits. It's ever so fortunate that we live in a civilized city as it is only there that all the new personal depravities are readily on display. It makes writing tragedy a breeze. Of course the people of the audience love it."

"So, what is the name of your next play?"

Sophocles is animated. "I'm not exactly sure but my working title is 'The Trouble with Youth is that it is Wasted on the Young.'" Alcibiades gives Sophocles a sly look and smirks.

Pericles responds, "that's a rather odd title, isn't it? Give us some details."

"It's an old story, pretty straightforward. Son kills father, beds mother, and wakes up with a headache."

Pericles is taken aback. "What? That's simply impossible, isn't it? Where do you get such ideas? Tell me just a little more, but remember that a child is present."

"I'm planning on calling this the Oedipus complex and then making up a new science and calling it psychology."

"What is psychology?"

Sophocles continues. "I don't really know yet but my soothsayer Bucephalus thinks it will be lucrative for its practioners. He says that they will be called shrinks, as big egos are shrunk to a more reasonable size. They will be able to charge big money for telling people that they're nuts. If they don't agree and refuse to pay you will be able to give them a pharmaceutical that will make them very happy and then just delighted to pay. Already on the market is a psychedelic laxative that lets you shit your brains out. It works wonders and most people like it a lot. It's like having found the fountain of youth. Very exciting, don't you think?"

Pericles asks. "Wait a second and back up. What's a pharmaceutical?"

Sophocles replies. "I don't really know, but something along the lines of a man-made concoction or a drug, or whatever, something like that, I don't know, maybe something like hemlock. I think it's got something to do with buying fake happiness and phony virtue off the shelf."

Pericles is perplexed. "Does it work?"

Sophocles says. "I don't know. I think it will work if you think it will. You know, that kind of thing."

Turning to Socrates Pericles asks, "Socrates, what do you think of such an idea?"

Socrates slowly says. "Well, as an idea I guess it's OK but fake happiness seems a little odd and that part about the Oedipus complex is a bit mystifying, rather childish, to be sure."

Sophocles continues. "Of course, it's all childish, that's the point. But really it's all about love, the one about the love of one's mother and the other about the love of money."

Pericles shudders abit. "Let's give the ladies a chance here. Diotima, what are your thoughts on love?"

Diotima has a rather crazed look and speaks directly. "Love is not anything that a man would understand. For the male, love is about immediate ejaculation coupled with brain numbing stupidity. A man is a rather pathetic sex machine that wants it early and often in as many ways as possible. This brutish lust they will call love but it is only violence to the human soul. Fornication may feel good for the moment to the humped up fornicator but it is nothing but a form of pure depravity. The sexual predators of the world may call that a sort of religious experience, that is their choice, but it is not, it is the worst in human despicability."

Pericles is amused. "Aspasia told me that you speak your mind Diotima but that was cutting to the chase quickly. Socrates, is that true what she says about male love?"

Socrates shrugs. "I'm in the army. It sounds right to me."

The beautiful and well spoken Aspasia says, "this may be true most of the time but not always. It is possible, after all, to do better and find in a companion not only sexual completion but also an intellectual understanding which we would call friendship. It is still a possibility to which we all may aspire."

Pericles smiles. "Very well said, my love. This is one of the achievements of Empire. As Athens has grown stronger it has been able to deliver a higher and higher standard of living in both quality and quantity that allows for the possibility of true understanding. The barbarians and Spartans, damn those Spartans, necessarily see love as nothing but brutish lust but we Athenians experience a much higher value, friendship."

Alcibiades has fidgeted enough and it is time to send him to bed.

Pericles turns to his ward. "Alcibiades you've heard enough about things that cannot concern you, so off to bed and sweet dreams. Enough of this adult prattle about nothing."

Alcibiades smirks and heads up the stairs to his bedroom. He partially closes the door behind him and sits on the floor, out of sight, to hear more, hoping perhaps to hear his name.

Sophocles is quick to say. "Boy, that boy Alcibiades is a handsome kid."

Pericles signs. "Yes he is but I have concerns. Everyone loves him too much and his knack for getting into trouble is rather acute. He's cute and all that but he knows it and uses it to get his way when perhaps it would be best to punish him. It's all rather difficult at times. He was just so young when he lost his parents, an emotional tragedy of the first magnitude."

Diotima cracks. "Prepare for the worst. Good-looking kids generally turn out very badly."

Pericles signs again. "I suppose but I hope not in his case. If he turns out poorly it could be really poorly. Socrates, I have a favor to ask. Alcibiades will soon be of military age and will need to enter the army. Since you are still on active duty, would you do me a personal favor and be his camp companion? Teach him well and perhaps your influence will keep him from turning out as badly as Diotima here expects."

Socrates sighs. "If this is my duty, I will surely accept but I'm afraid that you shouldn't expect too much from me. Little is to be done when the age of reason descends upon a boy making him a man responsible for himself. I will encourage but he will decide, and that is entirely up to him." Alcibiades sits behind the door, smiling, proud that he is the center of attention, confident that all will turn out exactly as he would have it.

Sophocles continues. "Pericles, you have such a great responsibility both in public and in your private life. I admire your leadership. No one else could be better at influencing the many to see the needs of the greater good. It was magnificent how you were able to get the Parthenon finally built. It is beautiful beyond measure. How did you get that to happen?"

Pericles straightens. "Athens is a great city-state. We must project ourselves fully to those around us. We manage a growing empire through the power of our will. The Parthenon was built to project that will to power. Imagine a foreigner coming to our city. Let's say from one of the islands that we control, and imagine him further seeing the majesty of that building, our Temple to Athena, up on the hill, upon the Acropolis, overlooking our powerful city. What would that foreigner think? Very little, but instead he would feel in his bones the power that is ours and surely not to be messed with. He would take that feeling home and spread the word of our overwhelming strength. To contest Athens is to lose, period. He would say to his fellow islanders 'let us pay our tribute to them and be happy that we still have our lives.' Such a foreigner would bow in obedience, or at least he should. Our policy towards the individual members of our empire is benign cooperation and they should see that. They need to submit for their own good, for we are the greatest nation on earth." Sophocles is transfixed, Pericles breathes deeply, Aspasia looks away, Diotima chews her nails, and Socrates is lost in thought, each expressing perhaps a different perspective upon this amplified glory of Athens.

Sophocles directs his attention to Socrates, who is startled. "What do you think there Socrates? You must have something to say. Aren't we the greatest in the world?"

Socrates reluctantly says, "excuse me a moment, I was a little distracted by myself. Yes, yes, Athens is great indeed but I think that everything is a bit overextended and I pray that it works out well."

Sophocles smirks. "It must, how can we fail? Surely you don't doubt the validity of Athens as a superpower."

Socrates continues. "Power is a difficult thing. Good intentions are often just a cover for easy profit. Others think otherwise and while Athens may seek the submission from others for their own good, those others don't always see it that way. Benign imposition often feels the same as tyrannical imposition. Some will resist submitting to our ideas about them. Trouble always lurks in the souls of those put upon by someone stronger. A superpower that gets entangled in its exulted opinion of itself is easily undercut by those not convinced."

Sophocles is dismayed. "By Zeus, Socrates, you are rather dismal about this. Pericles is right, the Parthenon is a great structure dedicated to our good intentions and you of all people should see that."

Socrates continues. "I agree with reservations as there are many opinions in the world and those opinions can vary greatly."

Pericles speaks up. "Socrates, you are a great man of perspective and I hope that you are just a little bit amiss, as I have tried my best."

Socrates says, "it's a little bit like being very good looking, (I read about this in a book once), as the thing goes both ways. The good looking never really get a chance to see themselves for who they are. Others clamor for their attention, making excuses when necessary, so the good looking can easily overlook themselves, knowing thyself not at all. Great disaster can often result. One can only pray that it all works out well when the chances are very slim." Pericles has his head in his hands, Sophocles is distracted by the wall, Aspasia looks mournfully at Pericles, and Diotima smiles pleasantly at Socrates.

Diotima asks, "Socrates, you are the only man that I ever liked and not because you are a man but rather because you speak without pretense. You tell the truth. Power is always power over someone and that someone can easily take exception. Life's a struggle and there will be winners and losers. To glorify one's own position is usually the first step upon the road to Hell. It's really too late for me. I must go. Socrates, would you walk me home?"

Socrates in earnest. "Certainly." The two look to Pericles, stand, and prepare to leave. "Thank you for a pleasant evening. I will do my best with Alcibiades but one day he will be his own man and make his own choices. He has great advantages and opportunities but there is no assurance as to the outcome." Socrates and Diotima leave arm in arm. Sophocles is asleep at the table and Aspasia leads Pericles away.

Pericles and Aspasia retire to their bed. She sees that the direct words of Socrates have upset her lover, the longtime leader of Athenian democracy. Pericles lies on his back with Aspasia draped half way over him on her elbow. They share an intimate and heartfelt kiss. "Pericles, I love you. You know that Socrates is well spoken but not always well taken. Your leadership of Athens is superb and will not be surpassed. Your understanding of the Parthenon as a projection of power is perfectly true. Have no doubts. I admire Socrates, living on nothing as he does, but he easily exaggerates and really knows nothing of the responsibilities of power. You, honey, are a leader of the greatest ability."

Pericles groans. "Sweet pea, enough of all that. I've done my best. The Parthenon is built, the Athenian navy is unsurpassed, the Empire is in place and pays, but the future remains uncertain. As much as it seems that things will remain the very same, all can be very different in a hurry. Damn those Spartans! I respect Socrates' views. Power does require submission and possible resentment but we are who we are, leaders of the free world and we must do what is in our own best interest. Short term greed can easily trump long term values as the fact of profit makes us less than we could be. To let go a tyranny, once achieved by whatever means, is unsafe. (2.63) (Reference to the Book and Paragraph of Thucydides.) We must live up to the fact of who we are. There is no other way. But enough of that now as my love for you is the only thing that I know for sure. Let us comfort each other and prepare for another day." They tightly embrace and fall asleep.

☆ ☆ ☆ ☆ ☆

Something like Pericle's dinner party would have been impossible in Sparta, the natural rival of Athens. The easy freedom and luxury of Athenian democracy would have been inconceivable to the hard oligarchy and regimentation of the Laconians. Sharing a common memory of consensus and alliance that so closely defeated the Persian beast, these two strains of Greek culture would find sufficient reason to fear and distrust each other. A great civil war was in the offing that would find plenty of reasons to engage in a battle that would reduce each to a shadow from which neither would fully recover. But the conservative Spartans had a perpetual and fundamental domestic crisis. Spartan society was based upon the labor of others. They brutally suppressed a resident population of Helots. A grinding seething hostility existed between the overlords and their underlings. One custom encouraged Spartan youth, on the threshold of manhood, to go out alone and kill an unsuspecting and innocent Helot. This was to prove his manhood to himself and to continually instruct the Helots on the proper understanding of their place in the world as under the heel of Sparta. These random killings were ugly and very easily very ugly. In a life and death struggle between a Helot and a Spartan youth, the youth could easily find himself dead. Family and clan outrage would be enflamed and hoplite troops marshaled to exact retribution. The Spartans were a brutal people, the very same as all others in this age of war and the rumors of war. Each fought for its own interests which naturally became entangled in alliances and partial alliances with others that easily led to an even greater violence. Spartan life was essentially the military training and marshalling to suppress a captive agricultural population that provided their life bread. The continued existence of the city superseded any individual concerns to the contrary.

☆ ☆ ☆ ☆ ☆

Alcibiades is now about twenty years old and is dazzlingly handsome. People crowd around just to look and are amazed, shaking their heads in disbelief that anyone could look so like a god. One could say that he simply sparkles, forcing people to look away, the very expression of the beautiful itself, as only a god could have intended. Be this as it may, little could be said for his friends, destined dead beats that could hardly match the pretty boy that so quickly learned to prey upon their self-conscious inadequacies. Alcibiades was the best gig in town though and the three, Dyclyssides, Rumshypocrites, and Georgiripides, would play it for all it was worth as they themselves had not the combined intelligence of an olive pit. To say that they would come to be thoroughly worthless would be a high compliment. Today they all have been drinking the usual fruit of the vine, as they obnoxiously are making their way through the various vendors in the marketplace. Up on the hill, high on the acropolis stands the newly erected Parthenon, but this gang's attention is fully devoted to making trouble, to being roustabouts for which juveniles are most famous. Their greatest satisfaction is to see people get out of their way as they push themselves through the crowded public area, the many deferring to the spectacle of arrogant youth and the beauty of Alcibiades. There is here the hubris of pubescence that comes to be reiterated in a low stupidity to which no one, surprisingly, has yet been prompted to say No. The great Pericles himself apparently can do nothing. Accordingly, this gang of four troublemakers remained free to spin their magic and the results can only be assumed to bode ill. They have stopped in front of the helmet maker, with the Temple of Hephaestus nearby, the shrine to blacksmiths and potters. The naturally burly blacksmith is pounding away on the finishing touches to the standard hoplite headgear and is reluctant to be bothered. Various other finished helmets are arrayed for sale. He takes no interest in the juveniles.

Dyclyss bursts forth, "hey Al, look at this stuff, helmets to die for, try one on, see how it fits! I bet there's not one big enough to fit your head."

Alcibiades snaps back, "Dyclyss, you perfect turd, don't call me Al. I'm Alcibiades, ward of Pericles, favorite disciple of Socrates, and most handsome man in Greece. Show some respect."

"Sorry, your highness, I forget again your special status. But try these on, you will be in the army soon and I'm sure you are ready to die to uphold your loyalty to Athens."

"Of course," Alcibiades says, "we all must fight to protect our city and our way of life, as we are the greatest city, the greatest democracy, on earth, but since I will surely be a commander I will be able to fight from the rear and direct the deaths of others. I guess I'll need a helmet at least for show." The blacksmith is a little perturbed but he then recognizes Alcibiades as from a house of money and becomes more receptive.

"Go ahead, try one on. Try them all on. They will make you look good." Alcibiades feigns reluctance as he always is wont to do and then easily gives in. He tries on three different types of helmet and with each strikes a pose as if he were a great warrior. There is a moment of awe as he seems to fit the part. He does look like a warrior, indeed. He strikes a Periclean pose and presumes to give a battlefield speech.

Straightening, Alcibiades lisps, "Men of arms, it is our day to show everyone that we are Athenians. Affirm your loyalty to your mother city. Cherish unto death the privilege to defend to the utmost. We are the warriors of the world that all barbarians must fear. Life or death, we fight for liberty. No tyranny can prevail against us. Onto Victory!" The effect is electric, his unique speaking skills impressive. A small crowd has gathered and is duly amazed. This most good looking youth is clearly destined for a place before the Assembly. The warrior's helmet fits well. People disperse as Alcibiades' group moves on to the next booth that is selling wine. A round of drinks is paid for by Alcibiades. The group gets up and moves down a side street, boisterous and still congratulating Alcibiades on his performance. Up ahead on the street there is an old man, slowly making his way, alone, as he turns into an even smaller side street.

Georgiripides, another worthless crony, says slyly, "Hey, Alcibiades isn't that Hipponicus, that old fart with the beautiful daughter. He walks around as smug as an old aristocrat. He always votes against the democratic majority in the Assembly, at least that's what my daddy says. Most people think he is a pain in the ass and deserves a beating. Hey, Al, I dare you to whup him. Just go up to him and pummel him silly. It will be great fun to watch. I dare you. How about it? Do it, do it! Someone like you can easily get away with it." Alcibiades responds quickly, a smirk comes across his face.

"You idiot, don't call me Al."

Dyclyssides encourages, "Ya, do it, we'll all watch."

Alcibiades is unsure. "It would be kind of fun and I'll only beat him a little bit, just so he gets the point. It won't hurt him much. Old men can use a beating once in a while so they know their place. Young beautiful people rule." Alcibiades quickly closes the distance between himself and Hipponicus who doesn't see the approach. Alcibiades pushes him from behind into the wall and he falls to the ground, hard. While trying to rise Alcibiades kicks him in the ribs sending him in pain back up against the wall. Hipponicus' face hits the wall and blood pours from his nose. Alcibiades' friends all laugh but soon enough they look around to see if anyone has witnessed the beating. It has gone much too far much too quickly. Others have seen the incident and are coming forward. The friends of Alcibiades start to move away quickly leaving Alcibiades alone with his victim. He then runs too as people come to assist Hipponicus.

☆ ☆ ☆ ☆ ☆

Alcibiades is distraught, tossing and turning in bed, sweating in profusion as he startles to consciousness, sitting up. He has done his cowardly deed and surprisingly feels remorse. Perhaps the good-looking boy has a conscience after all. He has clearly overreached, harming an innocent man for no reason at all. The displeased gods descended upon his sleep and forced him to a regret that would have very unexpected consequences. A youth as good looking as Alcibiades somehow is apt to find a way out, or others will have plenty of excuses just for him. He sits up, talking to himself. "What have I done? How could I be so cruel? What was the point? A stupid dare, from that Georgi idiot tag-along of mine. I'll pay for this. I must go and apologize. But how does one apologize for such a flagrant offense? It was so mean. But I must, I will go to Hipponicus and beg his forgiveness, even though I deserve nothing of the kind. I will go to him and let him beat me as proof of my sincerity. Yes, an eye for an eye, a beating for a beating. That will make things all better." His resolve is set, it is late morning and he leaps from bed. He shakes his head, sticks his head into a basin of water, refreshing himself, dresses quickly into a toga and walks out of the room. He passes a room where Pericles is hard at work, intently bent over some written materials. He is unaware of Alcibiades presence, who continues down the hall. Alcibiades encounters Aspasia.

Aspasia happily smirks at the handsome roustabout. "Up so soon young man? Boy do you look bad. Your late night debaucheries are bad for those good looks of yours. Someday I'm afraid you won't get your way so easily, but I'm sure you will learn. Where are you going in such a hurry?"

"Ah, ah, nothing. I'm just going to see my horses."

"Ah, that doesn't sound right. You always ignore those horses until right before a race."

"Ah, ah, then, I'm going to practice spear chucking."

"Whatever, of course it doesn't matter. You can sure make up stuff when a lie is most convenient. Your worthless friends get you in trouble again?" Alcibiades is not interested in talking with her anymore, turns away, and continues out of the house. He makes his way to the front door of the home of Hipponicus. After knocking loudly, a slave answers the door and is surprised to see the disheveled person of Alcibiades.

"May I come in?" Alcibiades blurts, "I'm so sorry. I must see Hipponicus, I must apologize, I must prove my remorse." The servant is not impressed and bars the way.

"What is this about? My master Hipponicus cannot be seen as he is resting and recovering from a beating he took yesterday at the hands of some cowardly little pisant kid. I'm on my way to the authorities right now to press charges on Hipponicus' behalf." Alcibiades bursts into tears.

"Please, please, it was me, I am that coward. Can I see him? I need to beg his forgiveness." The commotion at the door has brought Hipponicus' wife and beautiful daughter, Hipparete, to the room.

"What is it?" The mother asks, "what is this uproar?"

"Someone is here for the master," the servant replies. "He says he's the cowardly attacker." She and her daughter sweep forward as Alcibiades leans on the door frame sobbing. He straightens up and wipes the tears from his eyes, getting a better look at this gorgeous post-pubescent. The wife is both surprised and dismayed, the daughter attentive.

"Alcibiades, does Pericles know about your despicable deed?"

Alcibiades blurts. "No, no, he can't. He would be so disappointed in me again."

"Of course he would," she says, " and it wouldn't be the first time. You are an utter disgrace." The daughter moves closer, clearly intrigued, and perhaps entranced by this strikingly handsome morning guest.

Pleadingly Alcibiades continues. "May I see Hipponicus? I need to apologize and prove my sincerity."

"Well, he's very hurt, his broken ribs make it difficult for him to move and his nose still bleeds. He's in tough shape, thanks to you. Why did you do this? Hipponicus is one of the kindest men of Athens. This is a city of decency, a place of reason and law. He deserved none of this. Are you that mean? Are you a barbarian? And from the House of Pericles to boot? What a disgrace. It doesn't make any sense. Are you just a mindless bully?"

"Please let me talk to him!"

Hipponicus now appears through a door across the room, walking with a cane and holding his bandaged side. His nose is severely bruised. Alcibiades sees him and rushes forward, kneeling. "Hipponicus, please forgive me!" Hipponicus hobbles forward as Alcibiades reaches his hands upward.

Hipponicus in pain, quietly say, "What was that all about? I was just minding my own business as we are all taught to do."

"Yes, yes, it was all my fault. My friends just dared me to do it and on the spur of the moment it seemed harmless, just a little entertainment."

"Well it was no entertainment to me. You need some new friends." With this Alcibiades leaps up pulling off his toga and only a small wrap remains around his privates. He spreads his arms in the sign of the cross, tilting his head backward, his eyes closed. Standing such, the wife and daughter pull back in startled amazement.

"Please, beat me, beat me, now! I need to be given a hard beating."

Hipponicus is a bit perplexed. "Should I beat you with this cane? I can hardly walk. To raise an arm is sheer agony. But, yes, Alcibiades, against my better judgment, I will beat you." Hipponicus takes the cane and gently touches Alcibiades' arm. "There, take that, is that enough?"

Alcibiades is in tears. "No, beat me good, beat me like a dog. Beat me like a Spartan. I so deserve it."

"You shouldn't beat dogs or Spartans either, they're all innocent, but let's be done with this. Come sit here and try to calm yourself. You might give me a heart attack." The servant helps Hipponicus to a chair and Alcibiades reluctantly takes the chair opposite. The wife and daughter remain standing, the wife looking to her husband, the daughter to Alcibiades.

Alcibiades stifles his tears, wiping his runny nose with the back of his hand. "You're too kind. I am not worthy of your generosity."

'Perhaps not, Alcibiades, but there is no point to retribution. We are Greeks after all, not barbarians. I forgive you and, in a way, I am concerned for your welfare. Pericles, your benefactor, is a close personal friend of mine and we have spoken about your future. We both expect great things. I would like to take an even greater personal interest in your career. I offer you my forgiveness and my beautiful daughter in marriage." The wife and daughter gasp, one in horror, the other in expectation, as there is thought to be no better marital catch in Athens than the incredibly good looking Alcibiades.

Alcibiades gulps. "What?" A slight smirk surfaces. "Your daughter, this one here! Of course, of course, what a babe trophy, no, I mean, what a beautiful person. All for me. Thank you, thank you!"

Hipponicus pleased, turns to his daughter, "Is that alright with you Hipparete? I know it's a little sudden but would you accept? A marriage of the House of Hipponicus and the House of Pericles would surely produce offspring that would be a tribute to the city of Athens. By the way, Alcibiades, the dowry would be rather large, say 10 talents."

Alcibiades swallows hard, eyes bulging a bit.

"Yes, yes, of course, yes. I will have her for my own!" Alcibiades now becomes self-conscious of his near nakedness and reaches for his toga, quickly covering himself, as the daughter moves a step closer. They gather around for conversation and the servant is instructed to bring them all something by way of refreshment and celebration. Thus ended an odd episode in the life of our hero, something which was perfectly consistent with his character. His good looks got him his way, so easily. The marriage was duly consummated well enough, Hipparete quickly with child, but Alcibiades' regular debaucheries continued to the embarrassment of all concerned. Again, no one could say No to this natural bully. As a cocknotcher, there was no equal. In the privacy of his friends, with that little clutch of do-baders, Georgiripides, Dyclyssides, and Rumshypocrites, he was reputed as having said about the whole affair, "By the gods, it's good work if you can get it. Man, the money was good." After all, it was the largest dowry in Athenian history and a resource for untold misery to come. Hipparete though was saved the indignity of a life with Alcibiades. After giving birth to a son, Alcibiades Jr., her death soon followed.

☆ ☆ ☆ ☆ ☆

Alcibiades' character can be prefigured in other telling episodes of his youth. In a religiously devote society the experiences of youth are generally circumscribed by a natural respect for religious tradition, parents, and the dignity of others. Such was lacking in Alcibiades. Outrage is the word that most perfectly describes his antics. These were not the normal excesses within limits but rather excesses of a profoundly disturbing nature. Once he bought a dog with a particularly spectacular tail which he promptly cut off. Everyone was outraged. His comment was that "it ensured that people would be talking about him" and apparently bad talk was just as good as good talk, proving the adage that when one wants to be a star no publicity is bad publicity. It's all serves the good of self-promotion. Another time he found Pericles stressfully intent upon balancing his books to satisfy a public scrutiny. The smirking, lisping, young buck advised him that his time would be better spent being intent upon deceiving that public scrutiny. The dirty masses, The People, were not entitled to such accountability. Pericles was at a loss for words as how to respond. Where did such an outrageous attitude come from? It showed such an utter lack of respect and responsibility in someone so young.

One further documented outrage concerns his marriage to Hipparette. She sought a divorce and was required to appear in a public proceeding to plead her case. The Athenian patriarchy had little time and inclination for disgruntled wives and the proceeding was intended to discourage any such annoying charges. Wives needed to stay shut up in the home. Alcibiades rushed in at the last moment and begged her to reconsider and then carried her off on his shoulder to put her back in her place at the house. She was humiliated yet once more and he came off as some sort of popular hero to all the other abusive husbands whose wives had similarly legitimate rights to complaint. It was a spectacle that left few feeling proud, sordid is the word. Alcibiades got away with every single outrage of youth, his magnificent beauty conspiring to make his many admirers make way. Such an upbringing could only project poorly into his adult years, more of the same, to be sure.

☆ ☆ ☆ ☆ ☆

We Athenians have for long years received much acclaim for having stumbled upon the political theory of democracy. But, perhaps, "stumbled" is not accurate as this political innovation was the result of economic necessity, as in a time of crisis a political and social realignment was achieved that served us very well, indeed, perfectly. Of course, finally, this would mean much less as the force of circumstance, the results of war, veered elsewhere. Underscoring the special status of Athenian democracy is the fact that subsequently no other social community has been able to generate such a political reality, and in fact all cultures that have a foundation in something other than this democracy have never reached beyond political tyranny. The tyranny of tribalism, the power of the strongest, has everywhere else denied the possibility of the power of individual rights. Tyrants ruthlessly rule at the head of a tribe to the impoverishment of most others who are used up in the strife of mutual tribal annihilation. In stark contrast, the tradition of democracy has offered something essentially different.

Athenian democracy was born of a special economic necessity. Being a city with few resources and little domestic production, it was necessary to reach outward to other areas in order to gather for itself the material goods of survival. Situated within the domain of the Aegean Sea, the power to procure those goods would be naval. Hoplite land armies could protect the immediate city but to reach outward would require naval supremacy.

The Greek warship, the trireme, was 120 feet in length and 16 feet in width. Three levels of rowers, 170 men in all, powered the vessel in battle. Any one rower would know nothing of the battle raging beyond his narrow and cramped view, as below deck it would be just he and his oar in the roar of combat. Command discipline was essential. Through a series of drumbeats, specific instructions were sounded to the rowers who must then perform in perfect unison or all would be lost. Left, right, forward, back, stop, full speed, half speed, quarter speed, etc., were instructions that must be immediately executed in the confusion and chaos of possible imminent annihilation. Absolute discipline was the only hope for victory.

Navies of the day were made up nearly entirely of slaves. People were impounded into service without anything whatsoever to fight for personally, save bodily survival alone. Their function was to row under the threat of death. There could be nothing in it for themselves. Someone early on, an Athenian of acute powers of observation, recognized that if that rower had something positive to row for the effort would be better, perhaps immensely better. That something was political rights. As a citizen he was rowing for the reward of inclusion in the political process back home. Athenian democracy was consolidated of the rower's need to care. Having nothing to row for, a slave rower would never achieve the discipline necessary for final victory. The Athenian navy became invincible as the political structure back home included the rowers who rowed with a spirit of discipline and intention that ensured victory. With nothing in it for himself, the slave would lack the motivation, discipline, precision, and courage to win and would be easily overwhelmed by those who were fighting for victory for themselves, their families, and their city. Such is one of the constituting forces of Athenian democracy. In the sharing of political power everyone would be better off. Rather than serving the narrow needs of a political tyrant or oligarchy, the Athenians served each other and economic prosperity resounded. An invincible navy was the foundation of immense social, political, and economic benefits that rippled throughout society to the general good.

A similar paradigm fits equally well for the army. Hoplite warriors fought better when rewarded with political rights. Slave soldiers had as much fear of their own overlords as they had for the enemy. Confronted from the front and prodded from the rear, the slave hoplite had little to fight for save perhaps the blessing of a swift death. In other words, the natural limits of a narrow oligarchy or tyranny are simply unable to produce the necessary motivated manpower in order to command an expanding empire. The People needed to be included in the prosperity of empire, as a middle class for the first time stands at the foundation of political power. Pericles, the consummate oligarch, had the superlative genius to recognize this fact. Nonetheless, he equally understood that while the ever producing middle class was essential to expanding power, it still required strong leadership. Broad based participation would empower the city but still singular leadership ability would be necessary in order to stay the ever burdensome course of empire. Democracies will flounder in partisan stupidities if not led by clear executive leadership. Befuddled leadership would of course enhance the perfect storm of political self-destruction. Athens would experience both.

☆ ☆ ☆ ☆ ☆

Born of a maternal vision of having been sired by a lion and dead of the plague, Pericles lived a life as the most singularly accomplished Athenian of his age. Excellent as a political leader, military commander, philosophical thinker, astute negotiator, and consummate man, his legacy was sullied by a war that he so artfully attempted to avoid but finally was most responsible for its outbreak. In the democracy that he led for 30 years, he was subject to an annual re-election. Being an aristocrat by temperament, he gave guidance and leadership to a political body that must by nature pull in multiple opposing directions. He showed the citizens of the city the path to doing the right thing when their only desire was nothing of the sort. But, most importantly, he managed the Empire that sought neither unrelenting expansion nor onerous imposition. The wealth and prosperity of the Empire was the economic foundation of the greatest cultural formation in the history of the world. Simply, he built, in both material and mental ways. Perhaps the single greatest building, the Parthenon, was his creation. Periclean Athens equally laid the foundation for what would become science and technology, the arts and drama, and the very essence of a civil society that is the condition for any prosperity whatever. Of course, others would follow this fertile beginning and be more specifically responsible for these creations but Pericles was a fundamental initiator. He took guidance from the excellence which gathered around him. Anaxagoras, the philosopher, taught him the need to see true causality. An unhappy god need not be blamed when a material cause was obviously at work. Reasonable insight would necessarily be preferred to the fog of religious mysticism. Pheidias, the sculptor and maker of the statue of Athena within the finished Parthenon, taught him form and line, how to see clearly, how to discern an essential core that happened to be encumbered in a removable overburden. Sophocles, the dramatist of original psychological insight, taught him how to see into the dark motives of human beings, how to understand the common choice of irrational passion to rational accountability. He taught him how to manage a mob. Aspasia, his beautiful companion from Miletus, taught him the virtue of personal grace, the fulfillment of individual dignity, which allowed him to lead without seeming to push ahead, to let his reasoning carry the day through persuasion and encouragement when threats and intimidation would have been more readily expected.

The privilege of these friendships though paled in comparison to his own ability to learn from his own experience. His grasp of the essential totality allowed him to articulate the details in a way that was evident to most. But this totality is no settled reality, no set piece, but a moving target with evolving patterns of divergence and commonality. The overarching fact was the balance of power between Athens and Sparta, the one moving towards the future and the other yearning for the past, utopia versus arcadia, each with responsibilities and values that the other was ill-equipped to understand. The conflict that would be called the Peloponnesian War was long in the coming as the defeat of the Persians years before had already announced deep tensions, resentments, and potential jealousies. In building the unique economic powerhouse that was the Delian League, the Athenians took to themselves advantages that simply dwarfed the staid tyranny of Sparta and its Peloponnesian League. The Greek world had divided into two, something so natural as to be the central political template for all time. Neither side even cared to understand the full slate of concerns of the other. One was building and managing an empire and the other was managing its feelings towards that empire. Of course there was no absolute necessity that there is war. It need not have occurred but single steps move together in an inexorable direction until there is no turning back or, more specifically, there comes the point where no one individual has the courage required to choose otherwise and then the marching to slaughter can begin, a pattern infinitely repeatable throughout history.

Pericles may have been every bit as much to blame as he was not to blame for this war of unimaginable brutality. He tried to avoid it as much as he was its chief proponent. The Empire would be defended at all costs. In the multifaceted interactions of these two leagues, the Delian and the Peloponnesian, it was difficult to know what was what as motives and intentions became confused and misleading until error upon error delivered a reality that only a fight to the finish could square. But, mixing with this irrational brew was a perfectly perplexing asymmetry that all could see. While Athens was a naval power, Sparta was a land power. How to fight? Or, as it turned out, how not to fight on the other's strength? Had each been the same as the other, naval or land, but not one or the other, a single relatively small battle could have decided the issue. Such was not the case as each hid behind its strength and got no nearer the strength of the other, a stalemate from the beginning, plenty of time to pile the dead. Pericles succinctly stated the situation. "If they march against our country we will sail against theirs." (1.145) The uneven torque of asymmetry would leverage the war throughout and ensure an extended battle of attrition.

☆ ☆ ☆ ☆ ☆

My father, Thucydides the Historian, tried desperately to come to terms with the origin of this war. Matters of psychological intention became clarified as men of their own free will chose war. Historical necessity was as if nothing compared to the individual will to war. Any so-called "necessity" here is but another word for choice. It is infinitely easier to start a war than it is to end it on one's own terms. The Peloponnesian War, this "civil war" between Sparta and Athens, was a struggle between the power of restraint and the force of attack. In both camps contentious debates raged as each side argued its relative merits. Spartan society was ever in the preparation for war and yet ever reluctant to fight. Having the very best hoplite army, Spartan policy was cautioned restraint. But times were achanging.

Sparta had a unique kingship. Rather than one hereditary king there were two. This ensured that one could be away from the city with the hoplite army on training maneuvers or at war while the other stayed home to attend to political matters. With each new year the roles were reversed. The intention was to avoid the concentration of power in one person alone, to divide power to the better advantage of the city as a whole.

A Spartan war council is in session and King Archidamus is speaking. "Having just heard all the complaints against our enemy Athens, so eloquently presented by these ambassadors from our allies, I could be easily led to vote for war also, but a rush to judgment often misses the very obvious. Athens is a powerhouse. Easy victory will not be easy. They are strong in ways that we are ill-prepared to comprehend. While we are rightfully proud of our army, it is the Athenian navy that reigns supreme in the Aegean. In the time it would take for our hoplites to march to their city, their navy could have exercised force in any number of areas. They could easily sail to our rear, incite the Helots, and do much damage while our men are still enroute. Damn those Athenians! Furthermore, Athens is rich, immensely rich. Its empire contributes vast sums into its coffers to be used against us. Money buys hoards of destruction. I advise restraint. Let us build up our own resources before we take on this superpower. Let us negotiate and use the time to better prepare. We may need to fight but not now. Our allies are quick to implicate us in their own grievances against Athens but some delay here will serve us well. Vote No to war." There is a rumbling in the crowd but very little acclaim. Marsidides, a younger man of ability, leaps up as Archidamus takes his seat. He is sweating more than would appear to be necessary. He bellows forth.

"Old man, get out of the way. Your age has made you weak of body and feeble of mind. Athens is the aggressor in every way and must be stopped now, our future security depends upon immediate force. Our allies need us, our army is ready, and Athenians are cowards. Our honor depends upon it. Vote Yes to war! Let the Athenian tyrants feel the force of Spartan steel upon their weak and bloated bodies. We must stop those damn Athenians before there is no stopping them at all." There is a great roar of approval and the war vote is affirmative. A surging elation accompanies this final decision to act.

Spartan force then will be aimed at Athenian power, just as the gods would have intended, at least the Spartan gods. Restraint loses to attack and no one could possibly comprehend the pending losses. All tactical issues aside, the Spartans voted for war through fear and fear alone. The accumulating power and reach of Athens needed to be reduced before it was too late, before Sparta would be overwhelmed. A pre-emptive attack, preventive war, was to be the savior to Spartan values, or so it seemed at the time, on the verge of decades of disaster.

☆ ☆ ☆ ☆ ☆

A similar war council convened in Athens when word was received that Spartan hoplites in full battle formation were on the way to the city. Standing foremost though was the asymmetry, the military imbalance. The two colliding pugilists were powerful in diametrically opposed ways. One would fight with a superb land army while the other would respond with a superb navy. Each trying to get at the other would be an intrinsically difficult thing to do. Problems for each would loom from the very beginning, but the war must go on. Pericles, the long time leader of democratic Athens, has thought long and hard about this asymmetry and he gives voice to a plan for victory before the assembly of frantic citizens. "Word has come that the Spartans are on their way. While I personally have friends from that city, the most important being King Archidamus himself, be assured that my loyalty is absolutely Athenian. Our patriotic enthusiasm is of the purest kind as we all love our city. Our first responsibility to our youth is to teach them the glory of loyalty. Across the way the newly constructed and spectacular Parthenon adorns our skyline, proclaiming our pride and our power. But now, we are under attack and we must adopt a strategy for defense and ultimate victory. The natural first inclination is to gather our own hoplite troops and meet these Spartan aggressors on the field of battle. I could not more forcefully disagree. We would be beaten and lose the war in the first battle. Our army is good but it is neither as good nor as big as our Spartan enemy. Our strength is naval. Our additional strength is our walled city that protects both the city proper and our naval base at Piraeus. Our navy is unbeatable, and therefore I propose a strategy of defense. Leave our countryside and come to the protection of our walls. The Spartans will easily tire. We will send our fleet to the rear of Sparta, incite the Helots, and force the Spartans to retreat. Any Spartan attack upon our land will cause damage but never our defeat. We are strong in resources. Our treasury is full, our navy ready, willing, and able to execute a strategy for victory. Athenian patience and strength will soon convince the Spartans of their folly." A smattering of applause is evident as Athenians have come to naturally trust their longtime leader but such a policy is heartbreaking. To concede defeat to the Spartans, as it seemed such a strategy was designed to do, to give up the surrounding countryside, a rural domain of estates and well tended farms, to compress the full population within the limiting space of the walled city, seemed to be perfectly insane, yet that was the reasoned advice of Pericles and from his lips it seems right after all.

☆ ☆ ☆ ☆ ☆

A force of 60,000 Peloponnesians, led by Sparta, crossed into the Athenian landmass of Attica, spoiling for a fight. Athenian power needed to be humbled before it became absolutely invincible. Preventive war had been the choice of the Spartan warlords. The odds were with them, the asymmetry was against them. A short war could easily be won, a long war very much more in doubt. Pericles had anticipated this frontal hoplite assault perfectly, having already schooled the city on the proper strategy for defense. Concede defeat to the invaders at first and then send a fleet to the Spartan rear to inflict damage and encourage a Helot revolt forcing the retraction of the army in Attica. Bring all the people into the city from the countryside, safely protected by the extensive walls that enclosed the Acropolis and the immediate environs. Equally protected was the way to Piraeus, with long walls connecting the city with the naval base. The fleet could indefinitely bring in supplies and in the meantime the Spartans would recede back to their proper lair in the Peloponnesus more fully aware of the natural limits to their idea of dispersing the Empire. Damage could be done to the Athenians but equal if not greater damage in return would be done to the Spartans. The speed and destructive force of naval power would prove to be distinctly superior to the labored pace of a hoplite advance. The heartbreak though was the loss of the countryside to the land invaders as homes, estates, farms, olive groves, and all that made country life supreme was laid to waste. How could this be a winning strategy when the losses were so unbearably great?

Pericles won and he lost, the quintessential Greek tragedy. No man with such a stunning lifetime of success could have thought himself on his deathbed more of a failure than this masterful leader of the Athenian democracy. The strategy held and the Spartans tired, but the overcrowding within the confines of the protective walls nurtured the plague, which killed nearly a third of the population, Pericles included. Unable to account for unintended consequences, the Periclean plan of defense and limited offense failed and the war entered a new phase of both strategy and tactics. The new general on the scene would be Alcibiades. Periclean passivity would be replaced by an active war taken to the enemy. The brilliant career of Athens' first citizen had come to an end with the city fighting for its life.

☆ ☆ ☆ ☆ ☆

Athenian policy was as described by Pericles. Thousands moved from the countryside to the protection of the walls. Visible nearby was the Spartan horde of ravishers. Conditions became extreme as overcrowding worsened and then the plague swept through claiming many brave and innocent. The very successful Periclean policy of defense had been nonetheless catastrophic to so many. Nothing had been decided though as the war entered a new and even more brutal phase.

The Historian gave a precise description of the disease. "...people in good health were all of a sudden attacked by violent heats in the head, and redness and inflammation in the eyes, the inward parts, such as the throat or tongue, becoming bloody and emitting an unnatural and fetid breath. These symptoms were followed by sneezing and hoarseness, after which the pain soon reached the chest, and produced a hard cough. When it fixed in the stomach, it upset it; and discharges of bile of every kind named by physicians ensued, accompanied by very great distress...Externally the body was not very hot to the touch, nor pale in its appearance, but reddish, livid, and breaking into small pustules and ulcers. But internally it burned so that the patient could not bear to have on him clothing or linen even of the very slightest description; or indeed to be otherwise than stark naked. What they would have liked best would have been to throw themselves into cold water...Besides this, the miserable feeling of not being able to rest or sleep never ceased to torment them..." (2.49) "Strong and weak constitutions proved equally incapable of resistance, all alike being swept away...By far the most terrible feature in the malady was the dejection which ensued when anyone felt himself sickening, for the despair into

which they instantly fell took away their power of resistance…
there was the awful spectacle of men dying like sheep, through
having caught the infection in nursing each other. This caused
the greatest mortality…" (2.51)

Normal and lawful limits on personal behavior were gone.
With every expectation of imminent death, those living indulged
themselves in the most wanton behavior. Without a future, it
would be reasonable to live it up before one was slammed into
the dead of the past. "Perseverance in what men called honor
was popular with none…" (2.53) The natural restraints of
civil society were sundered in this descent in the direction
of perdition. What was witnessed was the first stage of the
dissolution of society and a return to the primitive, where there
could be nothing more than the savagery of daily survival, where
being dead would be far superior to being alive after once having
experienced the virtue of civil society. Only with the end of the
plague did this dissolution come to an end and people return
to their senses and self-respecting behavior. Sobering indeed is
the spectacle of human beings on the verge of final destruction.
Recovery was slow and difficult especially in the midst of war. A
testament to the resilient human spirit is that a near full recovery
was made and that civil society again stood proudly. Athens had
been tested like no other and had survived. In other times the
unique savagery of tribal wars may follow a similar template. It
will be a fight to the finish with no option for mercy, one tribe's
salvation being only the annihilation of another and on and on.
In the name of any god whatsoever atrocity will follow atrocity
until there will be the quiet after humans.

☆ ☆ ☆ ☆ ☆

Athens was the intellectual center of the Greek world, a
place of initiators and innovators. Artists, teachers, scientists,
technicians, and craftsmen from the surrounding region would

converge within the city limits to create something that may be termed a Golden Age. The dynamic interchange within this network of intelligence, this critical mass and path, was a work of art in its own right. Ironically, as so many came from other places, the foremost teacher of all was home grown and consequently rather despised, our booming and buzzing gadfly, Socrates. He was often to be seen and heard, discussing and pontificating on his ignorance on the way to a better knowledge of himself.

A diverse group of intellectual practioners have gathered for a drinking party, a symposium, and the topic of discussion is the nature of love. All participants have decided to lighten up on their normal wine consumption, agreeing to forego a descent into inebriation, the normal trajectory to matters of love, so that a more coherent discussion would be possible. We join them somewhat near the end of their subdued festivities and a young follower of Socrates is speaking. Pluton speaks, "Now Aristophanes it's your turn, no more delays, no more hiccoughs, as if that would get you off the hook. It is your turn to speak. The rule for this drinking party is that we do not get drunk, an innovation, to be sure, and everyone with an opinion must give a speech in praise of Love. So it is your turn and try not to be ridiculous. All we ever hear from you are insulting jokes that are usually in very bad taste, but this now is a serious topic, so don't hoot it up."

Aristophanes, always feeling himself a little put upon by these Socratic high-brows responds directly. "Well, quit accusing me! I'm innocent. Like Socrates here I'm just a humble observer of human nature, something always hilarious, easily a big joke. For example, with all this talk of love, what comes to mind for most people is a couple of goats in rutting congress in the field. Humans are not too far off, huh, so being a comic is just seeing it as one must. Don't fault me for making jokes. It's Socrates over there who is making the jokes, he just doesn't laugh out loud, it's all a private joke to him. He's always laughing behind our backs, pretending to be so serious, when it's all a big game to him, making others look stupid in public. Decipher that quirky smirk of his and it will lead you to the truth."

Socrates, the famous questioner stands his ground. "Aristophanes you're just a big kidder. Why pick a fight with me? I'm just sitting here minding my own business."

"And what business would that be, busybody? It's hard to believe a word you say, well, maybe just a few. You are after all a wealth of raw material for my dramatic productions. And, as you know, I always seek moderation, well sometimes, OK, mostly never, well actually, absolutely never at all. You win."

Socrates grins. "It's not a matter of winning, just of knowing, so why don't you quit with the drama and give us your knowledge on the nature of Love."

"Where were we?

Pluton directs him. "You had just gotten over the hiccoughs and perhaps you were not listening so I'll summarize the speeches so far. It will give you a moment to rationally organize your thoughts, hopefully."

Aristophanes rolls his eyes. "Good idea, huh, Socrates, and I guess I've forgotten already. Even just a little wine gets my opinions all in an uproar and of course they come out rather humorous, at least I hope. I'm just trying to entertain."

"One speech said that love is a giver of happiness," Pluton says, "another said a moral constraint, another a harmony, and yet another a bodily well-being. So if you are done dithering, give us your best, and don't be ridiculous."

Aristophanes perks. "Can I still be humorous? I need to be myself and can I make stuff up? Now don't laugh."

"Whatever. Get on with it."

Aristophanes expounds. "Well love is something that people once had, but no longer. It's because we're all a bunch of jerks. See in the distant past we were all One or at least some of us were One. I mean there were man and woman and then man/woman rolled into one. We were all stuck together. Let me draw an image." Pluton rolls his eyes, Socrates scratches his head, others look dismayed, anticipating more of the ridiculous.

Pluton shakes his head. "Go on. Cut to the chase?"

"So what we had was something we could call Circle Beings. Man and woman were stuck together all the time. One head, two faces looking in opposite directions, four ears, and two genitalia. The beauty was that they could run, I mean really run, chasing around, rolling forward on their hands and feet, cart wheeling like tumblers gone wild. They were fun to watch but they did have an attitude. They looked down upon the men and women that were not stuck together and then they took it into their head to look down upon the gods too. They were arrogant little bastards and they liked themselves a lot, two being one, and that was called love, stuck together for life. But things then got worse, love can't last." Two scantily clad flute girls come in to refill the wine glasses. Aristophanes leers at the girls and takes a swig and wipes his lips on his toga. Socrates has a bemused grin and the others are grimacing and shifting about but they do not interrupt the speech. "Are you ready for the rest? How did this love affair get worse? Easily. These Circle Jerks, as they came to be known, thought quite highly of themselves, as people in love are wont to do, and they decided to become gods. Just like that. Well the gods had other ideas and they consulted among themselves and decided that perhaps a little comeuppance for our Circle Jerks was due. The Jerks were simply cut in half with a thunderbolt and now they walked on two legs instead of cart wheeling on four. They were told that if they tried any more funny business they would be sundered again and they could then hop around on one leg. The huge wounds finally healed and thereafter they longed desperately for one another, wanting to return to cart wheeling, but alas, those days were gone. So there it is. Love is the yearning for a time before the Great Bifurcation when Circle Jerks cart wheeled freely and could do whatever they wanted. It was a time of bliss when they were as arrogant and full of themselves as they were stupid."

Pluton is stupefied. "That's a beautiful story, but what has that got to do with anything? Are you nuts or just goofy?"

Aristophanes blurts. "There you go. Insults aplenty. I tried my best, wishing here to educate the masses and all I get is ridicule. But, who cares? Socrates is still smirking so all is well. But Socrates, one question. If you strapped four Circle Jerks to a chassis and put some sort of motor on it and wound it up good, could you go lickety split and make it to the beaches of Atlantis for the weekend?"

Socrates ignores the question. "That's a good bunch of ideas you have! But sometimes a good idea makes for a bad reality and with questions of love the desire is to get a good idea and a good reality tethered together. The best example of this is when a beautiful body mingles with a beautiful soul. Rare indeed. Most have neither, some have one or the other, and a precious few have both, or at least that is what I'm told, I don't know myself. As far as your Circle Jerks go, it's an entertaining story."

"Socrates you must be kidding," Pluton replies, "but let's leave that stuff alone for awhile and now please speak on the nature of love. We are dying to hear your account now that Aristophanes has finished his story of the Big Jerks."

"Well, as you all know, I know very little, knowing for sure only my own lack of knowing, my special ignorance. Aristophanes thinks that I'm kidding but I really do know nothing at all but sometimes that turns out to be more, a little something, and not just nothing at all.

Aristophanes happily assert. "Well said, of course we know that you know more than that but aren't telling so when we let you know something you can make fun of us for not knowing more. Your not knowing is just a pretense to get others to publicly spill their guts and prove conclusively that they clearly are blithering idiots. It's a game that you play to humiliate others for your own amusement but, you know, they may get you in the end. There are many idiots in a democracy and they can easily gang up against you and quiet you once and for all. Beware!"

Socrates shrugs, "I don't know anything about that but I do know that I once met a woman, named Diotima, who knew something quite marvelous about love. Her account took me by surprise as I saw in a flash just how much I didn't know."

Aristophanes says abruptly. "Egads, something from a woman! What could a woman know about love? That's for men. Women are no better than slaves but they breed nicely. This is a man's world."

Socrates patiently continues. "When men treat women like slaves, it is no wonder that they look to be slaves but they are not. They are very much more than our own rather small minds can imagine. This woman Diotima was the smartest person that I ever met and for that I am thankful. She knew something and I listened with all my heart and soul. May I go on?" Pluton waves him on. Aristophanes settles back with a smirk. Socrates continues. "First of all, there is the mortal and the immortal, and the immortal wants to have nothing to do with the mortal. The gods think it better this way and mortals become desperate. They need something to serve as a messenger between themselves and the immortals, hoping and praying that these gods will take interest and save them from the mess that they have created on their own. So love is a sort of little god or a big man that makes his way in-between heaven and earth. He tries to uplift the one without bringing the other down, no small task. It's a full time job. What he brings back from heaven is a simple thing, the Good or the notion of excellence and harmony, beauty itself, something greatly in need of here on earth. For most people, the highest Good is the conception of a child, where man and woman come together and procreate a new being into the future, a sort of immortality, like the gods. But for some few, the highest Good involves going beyond oneself and finding a temperance and justice in the world in which we live. Love is the doing better for the general benefit of all others. Love is the seeing the world all as one, as the immortal and mortal are but differing perspectives upon the infinitely supreme same thing. Simple but difficult. Interestingly, even though the gods don't need to care, they extend this goodness to mortals as a dispensation that is perfectly divine. Love is a looking both ways and then always choosing to do the right thing, with no thought of oneself, or it is the perfectly egoless pursuit of the Idea of the Good which is merely the recognition of the being of an infinite force field wherein space and time constitute each other as an expression of an eternal velocity, a sort of $E=mc^2$, whatever that may be. I lay that out for your detailed consideration." Socrates pauses, collecting his thoughts, looking nowhere in particular when there is a loud noise at the door. A troupe of revelers barge in with Alcibiades in the lead with his sidekicks Georgiripides, Rumshypocrites, and Dyclyssides following close behind. All appear to be in advanced stages of intoxication.

Alcibiades shouts out. "Where is Agathon?" Alcibiades sees Agathon. "I meant to drink with you yesterday, so let's get drunk today. Oh, I'm already drunk so try to catch up. Drink to my drunkenness and be happy in love with the drunken." Agathon jumps up and greets the younger man for whom he has always had a desperate yearning infatuation, as older men were wont to do in this city of avant-garde relations.

He blurts, feeble and half-drunk. "Alcibiades I've loved you always. Of course, let's get drunk. Who has ever said no to the beautiful Alcibiades, the most handsome man in Athens? Beautiful of body and soul.

"Well said, I couldn't have said it better myself, although I say that very same thing often. Who is that over there, hoping to hide so I won't see him? Ah, my old war buddy, Socrates." Alcibiades plops down between Agathon and Socrates as Agathon bristles with jealousy.

Socrates cautiously, "Now behave yourself."

Alcibiades laughing, "Behave myself, surely you're kidding, you old kidder. But let's get serious. Can I drink to your knowledge of nothing? Socrates, you are one odd duck. I drink to girls and boys and then on to oblivion, and do the worse things that I can think of and wake in the morning clueless, with a headache. By noon though another gaggle of admirers have gathered and I'm off to the races. But, you, you, who are you? You drink but never get drunk, you're always there watching to help someone else as they stumble and fall. You know, it's drunks and children who tell the truth, everyone else tells puny lies to make themselves feel happy with all their greedy little lives. So, as I'm drunk, I'm going to tell the truth about Socrates." Socrates grimaces and looks away. "Yes, Socrates, here is the truth, I want you to know. You are the only one who has ever made me feel shame. I'm a drunken bully that everyone fawns on because I'm so good looking. I do the most outrageous things to both men and women, and they praise me even more. If I should happen to see you, you are the only one that makes me feel remorse for the awful things I do. But I can't help myself and it helps that I don't see you often. When you speak to me you are the only one to convince me to do the good, to do better with myself and for others, but it doesn't last. If only you had never existed, I could more shamelessly be myself. When we were in the army together, you helped me to become a better soldier and then you saved my life. I don't think that I ever properly thanked you for that." Tears come to Alcibiades' eyes, he sniffles, aggravating his lisp. He continues. "I naturally tried to seduce you on those lonely nights in camp, but nothing doing. All my friends are having the time of their lives and I'm stuck with you, rejecting all my well thought out advances as if that were the more natural thing. But, you know, those camp affairs were never love but only brutish lust that quickly became worse and were finally nothing more than disdain. But, with you, you are still hoping that I do better, you were looking towards the betterment of my soul, but of course you see that my faults are my own and there are always many new outrages to commit. After all, the most handsome man in Athens can only be expected to find the worst, it can't be pretty. It is all my fault as I know better but I can't do better. Socrates you are odd, indeed." Alcibiades sobs on Socrates' shoulder as the party begins to break up. His companions continue to binge, drinking from the half finished glasses of the guests.

Thus is told the story of one of the strangest friendships in all the world. Socrates, a man of consummate moderation and intelligence, and Alcibiades, a young man of perfect excess and outrage, each going his own way, each thinking much of the other, but finally finding just a few fond memories that were each one's own. One day, when Athens has been humbled, there will be a rush to judgment, to scapegoats. The name Alcibiades will leap to mind, and then the name Socrates, at whose feet the young Alcibiades sat, imbibing a fateful teaching that was presumed to go against the gods. This association will be indicted in the open air of judicial court with the results being that there will be still much more for the Athenian survivors to regret. The failure of responsibility is often shared.

☆ ☆ ☆ ☆ ☆

On a special occasion Socrates and Alcibiades had the opportunity to travel together to the Oracle at Delphi. This religious center of the Greek world was frequented by multitudes of people on pilgrimages to offer homage and to ask questions of the Pythian goddess in the hopes of receiving in return some small bit of wisdom, or a clue to the future. Not everyone would be happy with the comment received as in a manner cryptically bewildering things could go both ways. Perhaps the best and most famous example was the matter of King Croesus of Lydia. As King of a great empire he wanted more, as he thought it better that he take over his neighbor Persia. Being a large undertaking, he thought it best to consult the Oracle. Coming to Delphi he sought justification for his possible invasion and conquest. The question posed was, "Ought I, King Croesus of Lydia, start a war with Persia?" The whispered response of the prophetess left him ecstatic. "If you invade Persia one great empire will be destroyed."

"Oh, goody, goody, perfect, the Oracle bids me well. I will surely prevail!" He promptly ordered an attack and of course it was not the Persian Empire that was destroyed but his own. In his self-serving yearning to satisfy his extravagant desires, he didn't comprehend that it could still go both ways. Blinded by self-interest he blithered into doom. Invasion quickly gave way to self-destruction. The Oracle's prophecy was perfectly correct but the King's interpretation was a black night with no dawn, and he got exactly what he deserved.

The site of the Oracle at Delphi could not have been better. Situated in the central mainland it was easily accessible to most peoples. Halfway up the side of Mt. Parnassus, it overlooked a plush valley of olive trees. Ascending the Sacred Way, a path of respect and devotion, one comes to the Temple of Apollo, the natural centerpiece. Higher still sits a 5000 seat theater perched directly uphill and yet higher is set a running track that hosts the Pythian Games. Below the Temple reside the stone enclosures along the Sacred Way within which each city-state housed the wealth that was left as a rightful offering and compensation. Years later there would be discovered a fissure running underground the Temple that emitted a mind altering gas that the original builders must have factored into their choice of location.

Socrates journeyed to the Oracle in an attitude of devotion while Alcibiades, the young blade on the make, was looking forward to promoting himself or at least having a little fun at the expense of the local rustics. Central to his thoughts is the possibility of debauching the virgin prophetess. Of course no girl had ever said no to him so these religious mystics would be a proper test of their virtue and his vice, uniquely a game worth playing. Socrates would predictably disapprove but he need not know anything as keeping him ignorant would be part of the fun and the most natural thing of all. Their arrival fell between the end of the Pythian Games and the beginning of a dramatic festival. A few athletes remained as the actors arrived. Various performances were scheduled, both tragedy and comedy, so they would be able to attend and witness cutting edge presentations of social commentary, political wit, philosophical insight, and personal satire that was designed to leave one either laughing or crying. Socrates was reluctant but willing while Alcibiades was willingly enthralled as this very good looking Athenian had the opportunity to be seen in public, so that everyone could see exactly how pretty he was.

Before the unlikely pair would attend the theater, Alcibiades made a few bets with some lingering runners for a footrace. Being a superb athlete, Alcibiades had no doubt as to the outcome in his favor and he suspected that the prophetess would attend and with him stripped to the bare essentials, it would be his first thrust in the direction of her losing her virtue. He mused that when she witnessed him resplendent in the sun after an easy victory, a sheen of sweat glittering to his advantage, her heart would naturally go pitter-patter and it would be a quite easy matter to consummate the deed with his vibrant seed. In fact, he thought that it would be even more fun to make her wait, to let her sweat it out in female hormonal agitation. Rather than taking her by storm at the first opportunity, he would let her simmer and slow cook so that all responsibility for her denial of her sacred vows would be entirely her own. He would be able to claim afterwards, when authorities would be involved over this outrage against religion that he was entirely faultless, the whole mess being but the fact of uncontrollable female lust and moral depravity, truly great sport it would be. But before continuing with the possible exploits of Alcibiades it is critical to consider a conversation the night before as the two camped a day's walk from the Oracle.

Notwithstanding the younger man's pursuit of a radical version of egotistical hedonism, he, at times, under the gentle tutelage of his mentor, would wax philosophical and engage in intelligent conversation that was worthy of the highest praise. Here, sitting by their diminishing fire, tending the smoldering ashes, Alcibiades poses a question that goes to the very heart, the essential kernel, of philosophical inquiry. "Socrates, what is the truth, or what is the essence of true being?"

The teacher smiled at his favorite student. "How much time do you have? Of course I'm ignorant of the answer to this most profound of all questions but I do have a few surmises, a smattering of partial beginnings, that may or may not be of any use. And the problem naturally is where to begin. What exactly is it that one is looking for with such a question, and not knowing much at all, where is one to look?"

"Now don't be evasive, answering a question with a question is an excellent strategy for not answering a question against others but as friends we ought to do better and be as unquestionable as possible."

Socrates has retained his smile, "Frankness is a good start but insight is a tough finish. But let us work together and do the very best possible. We will need to stretch our imaginations to the limit in order to peer into mental dimensions that seldom see the light of human understanding."

The student is already perplexed. "Is it right to use the imagination that just makes things up, isn't the truth the realest thing of all, there to be seen straight away?"

"If that were the case," Socrates responds, "we wouldn't be asking this question as we would already have the answer. But the imagination is essential for any quest for the truth, as the real in any one example doesn't always include all that is possible and it is only with a grasp of the universally possible that it is seen what could possibly be real. The imagination, in other words, is able to set the highest standard for reality. Without the imagination, reality could be nothing more than the continual reiteration of the same over and over as one would blissfully suspect no difference at all. This would be the absence of self-consciousness as there could be no thinking to the contrary. Whole cultures exist with this limitation and even where the possibility of the imagination has occurred in fact, very few individuals would ever think to imagine anything at all, as daily existence doesn't necessarily require it, and values it not all."

"Wow," Alcibiades exhales, "that is a stretch as the possibility of the imagination then is nearly as difficult as it is rare."

"Exactly," Socrates continues, "so let us imagine a peculiar situation that may shed a little light on the matters at hand. Imagine, in passing, a cave, an underground cavern, with persons chained to the wall, unable ever to see anything at all but what is directly in front of them, not even seeing each other and this from birth for their entire lives. Continue to imagine an opposite wall, upon which shadows are cast, silhouettes of all sorts, which come to life due to a fire somewhere to their rear, the precise location again unknown to them. A passageway leads upward to an opening that allows in the light of the sun, adding to the shadows. There is always an echo that mixes the sound of one shadow with another leaving all in a greater confusion of noise and image. A trail passes by behind them down which walk a variety of persons with an array of things that constitute the cause of the shadows cast on the wall. They talk and jabber and catch the echo in a cacophony of sound that resounds like a bedlam of fanatics. These pathetic souls, something of which they themselves don't comprehend, never having seen anything different, have lived their entire lives so restrained, with their time being spent trying to comprehend these incoherent shadows on the wall. Reality for them would be a quite limited affair, but they wouldn't know that, knowing only the shadows as real, nothing else. That shadowed world is the ignorant condition within which we all live our lives, unable to discern anything but shadows of an unknown quantity and quality. These prisoners, while never having seen each other, would argue and rant and verbally fight over various interpretations as to the truth of these shadows, it would be all that they know. Sinking into quicksand would be a quicker way to the truth than this shouting about images reflected on a wall. But we don't see any of this. Our own lives are like this. Evidence abounds, as all the running around, chasing one thing or another, is but a competition over shadows that are mistakenly taken as real, a sad situation indeed."

"How can that be? Are our lives nothing but a scramble from one illusion to another? It all seems so real," Alcibiades said dejectedly.

"It takes the imagination to free us from this counterfeit reality to a higher insight. But let us return to our subterranean prisoners and see if any more light can be shed upon their plight, their rather dismal condition. Suppose for once, imagine, that one of these sorry souls were to be released, by whom we do not know, from his captivity, and then he gets up, pinching himself, rubbing his dysfunctional muscles, and then takes a look around. What would it be that would be the most obvious, the most startling? All the synonyms of the word flabbergasted would be descriptively accurate here. No greater shift of reality is possible, no greater transformation of the truth. All that which had been taken as real would now be clearly seen as unreal. He would see his fellow prisoners as something other than mere voices. He would see the fire to the rear, and the figures passing along the trail, casting their shadows on the wall and realize that he no longer need be deluded in his understanding of the truth. You could imagine that the release could be both ecstatic and depressing as he surveys the falsehood of his prior life and his new understanding. He would be perpetually amazed. But more is possible to this fellow of no return. Imagine further that he becomes aware of an even higher and brighter light and that a passageway leads out of the cave entirely, towards a luminescent orb further away, and that there is an outside. Words would be infinitely inadequate to his understanding and a pure bedazzlement would overwhelm his limited ability to comprehend. His eyes would experience excruciating pain. It would take some time to adjust, to begin to see properly for the first time. Edging towards the mouth of the cave he sees the sun, free and clear, and it is inconceivably gitanic, or very very large. Exhausted, our freedman would sleep deeply, perhaps dreaming this new world apart, reviewing in his mind the wonders of the day."

"This is a beautiful story but what has it got to do with the truth?"

"Very good question," Socrates says, "in fact, nothing at all." The image of the Cave is just an allegory that is intended to point one in the proper direction elsewhere. It occurs in the domain of the visible, the tangible, and of course the truth of anything lies in the domain of the invisible, the intangible."

"But if it is invisible, how do we see it?"

"It is necessary to more closely think this through and see that what is involved is not the sight of the eye but rather the insight of the mind, it is not a matter of looking but rather of understanding. Obstacles naturally loom large at this point. No teacher can take anyone beyond the limit of seeing to the unlimited dimension of understanding. Here it must be one's own personal odyssey. You have to understand it directly in a thinking that is all one's own, a thinking for oneself. As you are well aware, often times people catch me in a completely distracted frame of mind. I lose touch with everything but the special experience that is occasioned by this turn to the invisible. Of course I look goofy, but nothing can be done about that. Entrance into a greater world of essential things is sufficient compensation for being taken as a fool by those that can neither see nor understand anything. A preliminary statement is possible, if not entirely helpful, it must stand and be good until further notice. In the region of the visible the highest reality is the life giving sun that is the cause of all that is, as our ex-prisoner is astounded to see, but corresponding to the visible is the invisible where it is not the sun that shines forth but the Idea of the Good."

Alcibiades blurts. "And what is that?"

"That, my friend, you need to find out for yourself."

"But, Socrates, what is the point of all this? Will it make it easier to get ahead in the world, or to be applauded in front of the democratic mob of the Assembly?"

"The Idea of the Good is something that can have no truck with the visibility of delusion in our everyday lives. It could shed a truer light on things but no one would have it, no one would care to see, being quite incapable and unwilling."

"Too bad," Alcibiades continues, "as it sounds like it could be of some use."

Socrates collects himself and goes on. "To see how useful it would be let us return to our former captive and follow his career as he returns back to the Cave and the remaining enchainees and begins to enthusiastically tell them of his upward odyssey of discovery. He would explain to them that the shadows are illusions and that a higher reality exists behind and above them. They would not be happy with this information, not believing a thing he says. They would call him nuts, having lost his mind, and that he should get out of their way so that they can get back to the business of naming the shadows. He would be shown the door, so to speak, ostracized, so as to no longer bother them with talk of a separate reality. They may even bring him in front of the court on charges of corrupting the youth of the city with this dangerous gobblelygook that is as demented as it is useless. Our hero would no longer be very enthusiastic about anything in the Cave and he would perhaps choose to leave and live alone somewhere in the wilds happily convinced of the beauty of the Idea of the Good. He would have become a philosopher, a lover of wisdom, and infinitely grateful for the solitary privilege of understanding and truth."

Alcibiades is perplexed and showing the strain of learning. "That is all well and good but if the philosopher with his ideas is not able to force people to do what he tells them he's no better than a bump on a log."

"My friend this is not for everyone but only for those lucky few who are able to venture into the dimension of the invisible, that mental domain that is the source of all individual being, where there is such an awareness of joy that this is not only enough, but everything, a pristine Isle of the Blessed. It is the place where the gods are no longer many but One, where divinity is not separate but rather the perfect consummation of all that is. It is where theism, the distinction between God and world, is superseded by pantheism, where God and world are an indivisible totality. We may extend homage and devotion but then only from a partial point of view as our individual being reaches upward to embrace this unity. None of this can mean anything to you without traveling outside of yourself, without relinquishing the center of validity that is yourself, to a circumference of being that is everything." Alcibiades was already asleep, having dosed off a while back. The teacher arranged a blanket about the student's shoulders and then drifted off himself but not to sleep but to a place of divine dispensation, where all thoughts are as beautiful as they are rare.

Towards the rosy dawn, when all is afresh and the birds are twittering, Alcibiades is startled awake. Socrates is reviving the fire as the younger man blurts out. "In the name of Zeus I had a magnificent dream, all about birds of a feather."

"Good morning my friend, I assume then that you slept well."

"Yah, yah, Socrates I need to tell you about his dream of mine."

"Go ahead then, even before a bite to eat and a little refreshment?"

"Yes, before it slips away. I knew it to be but an illusion but it seems so real, as real as the day." The sun was beginning to overshadow the pale light of the little fire and its soothing warmth quickly dispelled the chill of the night. A beautiful day is on the rise that enraptures the whole world in a luminescence. But none of this would catch the notice of our dreamer as he needed to quickly grasp the fleeting chimera that was his dream.

Socrates assures him, "Please tell all as perhaps it may mean something more than we can imagine. Sometimes our dreams are a clue to a future destiny that begins as simply unbelievable."

"Well, it was all about me, me as birds. At first I was an Athenian owl, proud and regal, giving a hoot here and there for the amusement of lesser beings. Having, naturally, a bird's eye view, I saw everything and there was a great hubbub at Piraeus. Warships were being outfitted for some sort of naval struggle to come and everyone was happy and joyful over the prospects for war. Apparently everyone expected an easy victory that would be immensely profitable to some few. Then me, an owl, took flight towards Sicily but on the way I was no longer an Athenian owl but rather a Spartan eagle. It was an amazing transformation and I didn't know what to make of it. Then I was perched above a Spartan war council and no one looked at all happy, there were long faces all around. Talk was about war. The greatest hoplite army in the world was about to take to the field. Ever vigilant in martial training, ever reluctant to fight, this time it would be for keeps. A perplexing diversion amused me. There were everywhere little eaglets, hundreds of them, that kept chirping 'daddy, daddy.' But events quickly moved on and I next found myself no longer a Spartan eagle but a Persian peacock. I didn't look so mean anymore as I was as pretty as could be, the most handsome peacock in all the land. Female peacocks flocked to me as I flashed my tail. Times were good but it didn't last. Lickety-split I became an Athenian owl once again but as I was cruising the city, hoping to perch upon the roof of the Parthenon, an arrow came streaking towards me like a beam of light and nailed me right in the gentiles, a religious experience like no other, to be sure. It hurt like crazy but I had faith in my personal immortality until I caught a glimpse of a peasant woman pitching my beautiful head and mangled entrails into the sea as the rest of me roasted on a spit. What do you think, Socrates, weird huh?"

"Of course no one could know what it truly means but it had a clear theme as it was all about you in different plumage, interesting though."

Alcibiades responds despondently, "It had lots of action but the ending was rather too grim for my liking. Getting skewered is a bad ending for anybody, especially a good looking bird like myself."

"Enough about personal delusions," Socrates begins to rise, "let us walk on to the Oracle at Delphi and perhaps the prophetess will have some greater insight as to your surely charmed career." Off the two go, each in search of something that could only be a quite personal affair.

Pilgrims could get sleeping quarters at the base of the mountain upon which perched the Oracle but Socrates preferred a campsite out of doors but in deference to Alcibiades' wishes they took a room and were comfortably situated in doors. As expected, Alcibiades ran and easily won a footrace. He recognized immediately that he could hit on the girls with every expectation of success. Being so handsome was great work if you could get it and he got it perfectly. That night he slipped into the private quarters as the sleeping guard had been told to let him pass if he should so desire. He went about his business and was pleased as peach with himself, the girls had been savagely debauched, their vows of chastity shattered, and they too were rather pleased with themselves as well. Tomorrow he would seek prophecy with every expectation of good results.

Upon returning to his quarters, Alcibiades found Socrates seated cross-legged, lost into contemplation, per usual, with muted awareness of the things around him. Touching him on the shoulder, the sage startled but quickly reorienting his composure he asked Alcibiades, "How was your day?"

"Fun, but tell me what you've been thinking about? Anything new?"

Socrates smiled. "Same old same old but always new. I had a dream or vision, it's hard to say which, that was nothing like yours, no flying fowl, just a gathering of superb individuals whose only concern was the contemplation of the highest reality, the Idea of the Good, the idea that is the source and pattern of all else that is. There was talk of the beautiful itself, not beautiful things, justice itself, not single acts of justice, and love itself, not particular instances of loving. It is a world apart where the gods live and think up the being of the world."

"Nice, Socrates, I'm sure it was beautiful, but were there any woman, you know, something for one's personal amusement?"

"Certainly there were women but no one took notice as it is all the same one or the other. With ideas there can be no distinction of gender, as in this realm there is only a universality that by definition can only be one."

"Well and good for old people," Alcibiades retorted, "but not for me, it's all rather boring. Let's turn in early as the theater plays tomorrow, a tragedy in the morning and a comedy all afternoon. Ought to be an interesting contrast, crying and laughing, fake tears and phony laughter. Little to be learned but lots of entertainment and a chance for me to be seen in public."

"Those good looks of yours sure get in your way, always as vain as a peacock, but that's the nature of youth and someday there may be a comeuppance. Being a pretty boy may not always be so pretty." Socrates promptly falls asleep.

Alcibiades is mildly perturbed, thinks to himself. "This old guy is rather annoying. He sure doesn't respect my being so handsome, as he should, everybody else does. He's on a separate track, all his own and the act is really very tired." With this he falls asleep as well, dreaming about what no one would care to know.

☆ ☆ ☆ ☆ ☆

Before heading to the theater, the unlikely duo enters the Temple of Apollo to fulfill their appointment with the Pythian prophetess. The somber silence of the darkened interior quickens one's spiritual awareness and renders one receptive to the highest gift of all, that of prophecy. Making their way through a maze of side passageways, they find themselves in the final room of devotion. A few candles slightly illumine the shadows of the opposite wall as Alcibiades takes a seat on a marble bench, while Socrates remains standing throughout. A disembodied voice resounds throughout the chamber. "Who enters now and what is your business? It is better if you stand." The youth springs to attention, blushing, hoping this voice is that of one of his carnal conquests of the day before.

"I am Alcibiades the Athenian, come with Socrates the Wise, in search of the highest truth and understanding."

"Your reputation precedes you and little is said of any search for the highest truth as your desire leads into a much lower sphere, but for now your word will be taken as is. Being accompanied by Socrates is a presumption of sincerity so the Oracle is receptive to your question. What is on your mind?"

"Who is the most handsome man in all of Greece?"

"You may be wasting the Oracle's time with this one." A slight chuckle is heard that covers a quick laugh. "That hardly concerns the highest truth but for you perhaps it is. The answer may surprise you as the obvious answer is that the most handsome man in all of Greece is clearly your companion here Socrates."

Alcibiades is dumbfounded. "What? Socrates isn't even pretty, anybody can see that, are you blind as a bat or just stupid."

"Not needing to take issue with your rudeness and lack of respect for the persons of this Temple, a simple statement is possible. Oftentimes things are the very opposite of appearances. You are surely very handsome in body but your attitude towards others is truly poor and, one could affirm, ugly. You are a depraved individual that is intent upon personal gratification at the expense and dignity of others and your activities will always spell disaster wherever you happen to be. That cannot be a definition of handsome. Socrates, on the other hand, your teacher and guardian angel, has the most exulted spirit, always in search of the higher rather than the lower, the pristine rather than the contemptible. Nothing could be more handsome than that. You lose. To keep you from crying over this, something very embarrassing to all things, the Oracle will allow you to ask a second question, a rare dispensation indeed."

Alcibiades is not happy, the little slut had a lot of gall with her preaching about the beauty of the old plug Socrates. He blurts, "Should I enter politics?"

"Is it always about you? I suppose that can only be expected with your level of perfected narcissism. But the answer is so clear and easy that it will be very quick to conclude this session. Great events will surround your political activities and matters of war will be decided. Your loyalty will be tested and proven to be extremely wanting and in your wake there will only be disaster. Many will die from your vanity."

"What is that supposed to mean? Talk straight!"

"The Oracle always talks as straight as is possible, it is for you to take careful notice and interpret well. Most do this very poorly as they themselves get in the way. It would seem that you will follow the norm. Only a strict adherence to personal accountability and integrity will help you now as you stand on the verge of the perfectly helpless. Go forth and decide for yourself. The damage that you have done here is already too reprehensible to contemplate. Be off with you and never return." The two leave the premises, with Socrates never having said a word, infinitely concerned for his young friend who was surely destined for no good. Out of the Temple they crossed over the 20 paces to the Theater and a crowd has already gathered and heads turn and murmurings amplify as the handsome Alcibiades makes his entrance. A foul scowl still graces his countenance as curtain time is at hand. News of his temple debaucheries has yet to be rumored. It may be time to get out of town but not yet as the play begins. *The Oresteia* by Aeschylus is the production.

The dramatic action of the play can be summarized. King Agamemnon is faced with the choice between signaling the start of the fleet's passage to Troy in order to avenge the abduction of his brother's wife Helen, an act that simply must be undone, and the sacrifice of his daughter in order to appease a god that refuses to allow the winds to blow until that god's brutal demand is met, an act that simply cannot be done. Agamemnon's choice is between fulfilling his responsibilities as king and renouncing his fatherhood in order to placate the demands of a god. He must choose the death of his daughter in order that the slaughter at Troy may begin. This is an impossible choice that requires decision nonetheless. Heartache and then heartbreak are the necessary wages for these deeds of choice that can only be one's own. The voice of the heartache of tragedy is clear. A smattering of verse will do. "It means victory with a twist…you can expect the anger of heaven." "Agamemnon heard the terror stirring and looming through the words of the seer. But he was no longer a man in a man's body confronting the lonely fate that would kill him. He was a war-machine, a launched campaign, a whole nation of vengeance." But deep trouble is foreboding. "At that point Calchas the seer spoke of Heaven. He told us what had to be done to shift the wind—when they heard what Artemis demanded the warlord cried out, incredulous…if I obey the goddess, my own daughter must die. If I deny the goddess, this whole army has to dissolve." "If I obey the goddess, and kill my own daughter—what do I become?" He answers for himself. "The King of cruelty. Painting my royal palace afresh with her blood, the blood of Iphigenia." His decision is made. "So the great king, Agamemnon, launches his thousand keels on the blood of a virgin. To reclaim a stolen whore. Iphigenia for Helen. He takes what he wants—and pays for it." "Her father gives the signal. Iphigenia is hoisted off her feet by attendants—they hold her over the improvised altar like a struggling calf. The wind presses her long dress to her body and flutters the skirt, and tugs at her tangled hair—'Daddy!' she screams. 'Daddy!'—her voice is snatched away by the boom of the surf." And now the deed has been done and woe to the House of Atreus, the domain of Agamemnon. The soul becomes twisted onto itself and the compression of heartache warps the natural coordinates of space and time into an inner maelstrom of rage and fury. Events continue apace with the annihilation of Troy. "The happiest day and the worst moment collide and grapple, on skidding feet, in the uproar of a slaughterhouse. The women of Troy are a population of mourners." But atrocities in a foreign war are soon to be visited upon the homeland. And home is where Clytemnestra, Agamemnon's wife, mother of Iphigenia, awaits, brooding a dark future, harboring a righteous revenge. The ten year long absence of the King, husband, and child killer has left her to the guile of a new bedmate, Aegithus. Enamored co-conspirators welcome the great King home with his death, a homecoming straight to the grave. "Revenge begets revenge, truth spins and evaporates as blood drains from the head." Aeschylus carries on in a continuing vein. Vicious act follows upon vicious act, all justified in a way suitable to each perpetrator in turn. Agamemnon kills Iphigenia, Greeks kill Trojans, Clytemnestra kills Agamemnon, Orestes, son of Agamemnon and Clytemnestra, kills Clytemnestra and Aegisthus, and Orestes finally is taunted by the Furies, the demons of the imagination, who seek justice. Equally entangling, Helen is the sister of Clytemnestra as Menelaus is the brother of Agamemnon. Brothers marry sisters to spawn a fury of vengeance. Collapsing circularities will ensnare all in a rush to perdition. But a darker secret underlies even this, no one is innocent, guilt is universal, save Iphigenia. There is a "family tree of murder." In the family's past, an apparent resolution was agreed upon and a banquet offered. Atreus though nurtured other intentions for a final revenge. Aegisthus speaks.

"He took my two brothers, the two eldest sons of Thyestes, cut their throats and bled them, butchered them, and stewed the meat. The feet with their toes, the hands with their fingers he hid at the bottom of the dish. Over those he layered the steaks and collops, the chopped livers and kidneys, the hearts, and brains… This was the dish set steaming before the father. He had gorged himself, to honour the feast, before he discovered what he was swallowing. When he recognized it, when he saw the hands and the feet he fell backwards, vomiting over the floors his own children. He kicked the table over, and as the bowl shattered he screamed out this curse—to earth and to heaven and to hell he screamed it: 'Just as this bowl shatters so let the whole lineage

of Atreus be shattered and spilt.' Aegisthus kills to avenge his
brothers, Clytemnestra kills to avenge her daughter, Orestes kills
to avenge his father, and on and on as the cycle of homicide
revolves. Heartache is the common coin of the royalty of the
Kingdom.

This pitiful descent into perdition leaves one breathless.
Socrates and Alcibiades return to their quarters exhausted
and cathartic, purged of all but the blackness of unjust justice
delivered, the night with no dawn. Alcibiades collapses on the
bed as Socrates refreshes himself with a drink of the mountain
spring nearby. The afternoon's entertainment will at least not be
so bleak as any comedy of the poet Aristophanes is full of laughs.
Rumor has it that a cameo appearance by a character depicting
Socrates will be presented and that to Socrates the man can only
mean trouble. Aristophanes will be sure to reduce the Athenian
gadfly to a blithering idiot. But nothing is better for the soul than
laughter even if it is at one's own expense. A power nap and off to
the theater for round two.

In *The Clouds* Aristophanes offers a caricature of Socrates.
The great philosopher of thinking is made to be the buffoon. The
thinker that reaches to the Heavens for truth is entangled in the
clouds of a more immediate earthly proximity. A father, become
dissolute, despondent, and debt-ridden due to the horse driven
misdeeds of his son, hopes for relief. Reform of the youngster
can proceed apace at the Thinkery of Socrates where he can
learn "the technique of Winning a Lawsuit." The father's debts
will be forgiven when his son wins in court against the father's
creditors, so he hopes. Of course, with much yet in arrears there
is equally much yet to go awry. The son is not impressed. He
is already familiar with this school of learning. They are "filthy
charlatans…frauds…barefoot pendants with the look of death."
And Socrates is but a humbug. So the boy resists education but
his father implores him to re-consider and go and learn the special
Socratic Logic. "…if you can learn this…Logic, I wouldn't have
to pay a penny of all those debts you've saddled me with." The

listener is already quite amused. The presumption of impossible expectation as a last resort is funny to all but the debtor. If the son refuses education then the father is willing to give it a go. He is admitted to the Thinkery in the midst of major investigations. Under consideration is a theory of the gnat and how it "tootles" or makes a noise. The Socratic Theory is insightful.

According to this, the intestinal tract of the gnat is of puny proportions, and through this diminutive duct the gastric gas of the gnat is forced under pressure down to the rump. At that point the compressed gases, as through a narrow valve, escape with a whoosh, thereby causing the characteristic tootle or cry of the flatulent gnat…So the gnat has a bugle up its ass.

The father is impressed with the breadth of the analysis. "Why, the man who has mastered the ass of a gnat could win an acquittal from any court." The father is allowed entry into the Socratic inner sanctum and is obviously awed. Socrates is suspended high overhead in a basket and shouts down to explain his position.

"You see, only by being suspended aloft, by dangling my mind in the heavens and mingling my rare thought with the ethereal air, could I ever achieve strict scientific accuracy in my survey of the vast empyrean. Had I pursued my inquiries from down there on the ground, my data would be worthless. The earth, you see, pulls down the delicate essence of thought to its own gross level."

The father though is in a pinch for time and does not want the stuff of the empyrean but rather the stuff that will win in court. He wants the "get-away-without-paying argument." Of course he will pay "any price" for this. But Socrates is undeterred and pleasantly pontificates in the manner of philosophers.

"Come forth, be manifest, majestic Clouds! Reveal your forms to me. And whether on Olympos' snow your brooding eyrie lies, or on the waves you weave the dance of Ocean's lovely daughters, or dip your golden pitchers in the waters of the Nile, or hover on Mount Mimas' snows, or over Lake Maiotis—come forth, great Clouds! Accept our prayers! O hear us! Amen."

The father's education deepens. He learns of the true nature of clouds, they are goddesses and patrons. "Clearly then you must also be ignorant of the fact that the Clouds are also patrons of a varied group of gentlemen, comprising: chiropractors, prophets, longhairs, quacks, fops, charlatans, fairies, dithyrambic poets, scientists, dandies, astrologers, and other men of leisure. And because all alike, without exception, walk with their heads among the clouds and base their inspiration on the murky Muse, the Clouds support them and feed them."

After a few more questions, the father needs to pass a test. "Sir, if you can pass our test, we guarantee that you shall be the cynosure of Hellas. Our requirements are these: First is your memory keen? Do you hanker for researching? Are you subject to fatigue from standing up or walking? Does winter weather daunt you? Can you go without a meal? Abstain from wine and exercise? And keep away from girls? Last, do you solemnly swear adherence to out code? To wrangle, niggle, haggle, battle, a loyal soldier of the Tongue, conducting yourself always like a true philosopher."

The father's initiation begins and he is on his way to becoming a philosopher. "Do any damn thing you've a mind to, my only conditions are these: that when the ordeal is completed, a new Strepsiades (the father) rise, renowned to the world as a Welsher, famed as a teller of lies, a cheater, a bastard, a phoney, a bum, shyster, mouthpiece, tinhorn, scum, stoolie, con-man, windbag, punk, oily, greasy, hypocrite, skunk, dunghill, squealer, slippery Sam, faker, diddler, swindler, sham, or just a plain Lickspittle."

Enough is enough. The point has been made. The juxtaposition of Socrates the philosopher and him as the buffoon is amusing and laughable. The serious is undercut by the ridiculous, the ponderous by the hilarious, and the joke is infectious. *We laugh together.* As tragedy is an implosion unto oneself, hilarity is an explosion outward to others.

The literary portrayal of heartache and hilarity may say much about the Greek accomplishment. Sundered inward with the one and catapulted outward with the other, a tension of opposition, a dialectic of sorts, is created that may seek some sort of reconciliation, some resolution. The suggestion is that the full force of self-consciousness is born with the personal effort of this reconciliation that may or may not reach to completion. These two forces, the heartache of tragedy and the hilarity of comedy, shattered the imposition of political tyranny upon the self, and announced a *brave new world* of personal choice and individual initiative. The limits of human possibility have just been greatly expanded, transformed into the dimension of creativity, accountability, initiative, democratic social participation, and finally the Socratic Delphic dictum to Know Thyself. The odyssey of the Western Spirit has just been given direction, impetus, and configuration. The possible has been constituted and while actuality and reality will lag far behind, in time, it will have had the most privileged beneficiaries. Stated otherwise. In the nexus of Aeschylus and Aristophanes, tragedy and comedy, will be constituted the unique experience that will create the possibility of choosing to Know Thyself. This is a cultural achievement ripe with enthralling possibility and ominous with deadly danger. Locating the balancing center, the in-between, of moderation, will be monstrously difficult and easily prone to the excesses of the achievement itself. Within the dynamic of success is equally found occasion for failure.

☆ ☆ ☆ ☆ ☆

Socrates rose early the next morning, leaving Alcibiades longer to his dreams, hoping to make a special pilgrimage to a shrine at the very top of Mt. Parnassus. Few bothered with this difficult trek directly uphill as the Temple of Apollo was usually deemed a sufficiently religious experience and that none further would be needed. But, after a full day at the theater, among the push and pull of social stress at its tragic and comedic worst, a day alone on the mountaintop would provide a solitude that could perhaps go far towards being himself, simply at peace, adjusting himself to his inner voice. He had been told that there was a tangled and tortured path to the top that started below at the back of the running track that stood just above the theater that fronted the Temple of Apollo. Traveling upward throughout, Mt. Parnassus demanded a physical effort that few would freely choose but Socrates was certainly adequately fit for the task. It would all be a happy challenge to the summit and then there would be the panorama view that extended out in all directions in a visual sweep that was like none other. As he crossed the running track in the morning chill towards what he thought to be the start of the trail there was a small boy sitting upon a rock. Socrates was a bit startled as if the boy knew that he was coming and that he may need some guidance. The boy leaped to his feet as Socrates approached. "Good morning Mister Sir, may I help you to get to the top?"

"Well, of course," Socrates replied, "but how is it that you are here today to assist me, as if you were waiting just for me?"

"I live in these woods on the side of this mountain and I just know what I need to know and anyone coming here, at this time, alone, needs my help."

"What is your name?"

"They call me Pan. I'm a shepherd up here with a herd of twenty goats. There are all around, would you like to meet them?"

"Of course."

Pan whistles sharply and within minutes his twenty goats have assembled, each vying for his personal attention. The affection was mutual. One nuzzled Socrates garment and leaned its head against his leg. Never had he witnessed such a display of care, person to animal, animal to person, sentient being to sentient being. After awhile Pan whistled again and they all promptly left in different directions, each seeking out its special place to sleep the day away. "Do you live in the village below with your parents?"

"My parents are dead. A bunch of men came through one day, calling themselves Athenians, whatever that is, and killed all the men of the village, including my father. A little later a bunch of men calling themselves Spartans came through, whatever that is, and finished off my mother. They tortured her for hours, jumping up and down on her, one after another. She screamed a lot, I don't know why they didn't just kill her, and then she was dead. I loved my mother and she loved me. I watched her die and then escaped to the woods. The nice princesses of the Temple help me once in awhile with food but I stay outside mostly and sleep in a cave that is home to me. I don't like people."

Socrates is moved by the depth of the boy's anguish. "My gosh, how sad, how very sad, I'm an Athenian myself. You must hate me and wish me harm."

"No, not at all, you were not one of them, it is no fault of yours. Nothing means much to me anymore and I have no idea what all of this could mean, killing and killing some more. It makes no sense to me. I have my goats and that is enough for me. When I look into their eyes all I see is innocence and love and that is all that matters to me. When I saw those men kill my father and mother I lost myself. If I never find myself again I will be very happy."

Socrates is deeply touched by the overwhelming loss for a boy so young and now alone. His almost divine attitude is equally mystifying. How could such a little boy who has suffered so much still find an encompassing kindness? "Young man, let us talk later, but for now lead the way up the path to the top of the mountain."

Pan leaps forward. "Yes sir, follow me." With that he was off as Socrates hurries after. The climb was long and twisted, one way then another, perfectly zigzag, as there was no straight line anywhere. Huffing and puffing, Socrates was exhausted after awhile but Pan kept ahead. "Just a little further and we can rest at a mountain spring. The water has magical powers, the goddesses at the Temple say so. It will revive you in no time."

"Thanks so much, I need something soon or I'll give out."

"Don't worry. You're the toughest old guy yet, most have already turned back." The running water appeared and the two drank deeply, sitting down on a stone ledge that held back a small pool of water.

After a short respite, Socrates spoke up. "Will you always live on the mountain or will you find someplace to live in the village?"

"The village is no place for me, I want none of it. I will stay here on the mountain, where there is forest, wind, rain, sunlight, and, of course, my goats. They will protect me. They alert me when anyone sets a first step in this domain. I have no desire to live any way other than the way before me now. This is all and everything to me and solitude is my final comfort."

The clear and articulate expression of the boy was something to behold, seemingly out of character with his youthfulness. No child ought to have such a sense of awareness and expression so mature in years. He suffered much for this, but loved more, so that was perhaps his happiness. Who could suggest otherwise? Socrates spoke, "I find myself so quickly refreshed, let us continue to the top." The two were afoot again and in no time stood at the summit. Socrates looked around, turning in a complete circle and everywhere there was a vast distance of perspective, like none that he had ever seen. It was like seeing the whole world at once. The pristine clarity of the atmosphere extended one's view yet further. To the south there was the Corinthian Gulf and far beyond the land of the Peloponnesus and all around there was a view that left him planted in awe, a spectacle of the highest magnitude.

Pan lifted his left arm in a sweep across. "This is what I live for, this view that beholds the gods."

Socrates drifts into thought. In the glorification of the gods, there was opened up the division between the immortal and the mortal, between the divine and the worldly, the vastness of which if fully comprehended is nothing less than the religious experience itself. The gods occupied an infinite domain of perfection, as man occupied a finite domain of imperfection. One worshipped across this chasm. Standing in the worldly, one reached upward into the Holy. Such was the religious experience of theism, the gods distinctly apart from man who worships from below. Standing with Pan, holding lightly his tiny hand, looking across the way, it was not division but rather unity that one most fully understood. The full being of the world, as partially present here in the vista at the top of Mt. Parnassus, was a single unity that did not leave man apart but rather a full participant in the single totality. This was not the theism of a god apart but rather the Pantheism of a God all in One. Parmenides may be right. All is One or One is All, is singularly the perfect expression of the full Being of the world. The personal love of the world by the boy Pan may have been the most perfect expression of the perfection of the unity of God and world. Simply being here was the ultimate experiencing and witnessing of this incommensurable Revelation. Socrates would be forever eternally grateful for having stumbled upon this journey upward with a little boy as hallowed as he was wise.

They continued to witness the view when an indistinct murmur emanated from somewhere, gradually getting louder and louder and then he realized that it was Pan chanting. "Om mani pedme Hung, om mani pedme Hung," and on and on. Socrates followed the boy's lead and then chanted the same words for perhaps hours. Finally the boy quit speaking and they looked at each other.

Socrates speaks first. "How beautiful! What was that?"

"I don't know, but one day it just came to me from afar and it always leaves me happy. Did you like it?"

"Why yes indeed, it clears the clutter and allows one to see a reality that is without me, a psychological dimension that just floats along, never being tethered to anything here and now. I suppose it is the freedom to which we yearn but without that having anything to do with the world. It is the mental transformation that allows one to enter the spirituality common to the mystic but superlative to us lesser mortals."

Pan smiles, "Well I hadn't thought of any of that, but it sounds right, I suppose. I just live it. It lets me think I have a mother and father without crying. They still live because they once did and they still love me, I know, somehow, and here at the top of the mountain, they see me clearly and my love for them is bigger than the world, as immortality is for everybody. If any Athenians or Spartans return, I will let them know that there is no one left to kill and that they can have whatever they want. They of course won't come up the mountain, so me and the goats are safe. It would be like nothing to spook the wits out of them and they won't ever see a thing."

☆ ☆ ☆ ☆ ☆

While Socrates was a home grown intellectual agitator, there were many more who came from afar, traveling to the Athenian center proposing to enlighten us in the proper understanding of the truth, specifically for cash. These Sophists, as they were called, dispensed wisdom in a cash-value exchange that was not always entirely satisfying to entirely everybody. One such great teacher was Parmenides, reputed to be not a day less than 137 years old. He had agreed to meet with Alcibiades and his companion knuckleboneheads, Dyclyssides, Rumshypocrites, and Georgiripides. Parmenides had begun to crumble as he is nearly deaf and hears only what he wants to and surely mostly blind as he sees very little as well. His voice is still strong though and for immediate payment he can make up most anything on the spot. These young bucks would be none the smarter if a bit more impoverished with the encounter. After all it was just daddy's money anyway. Alcibiades reverently begins, "Parmenides, it is our esteemed privilege to talk with you. My three friends here, Dyclyssides, Rumshypocrites, and Georiripides follow me everywhere, looking for handouts, and supporting my career. Everybody with a future needs an obedient entourage, this is mine. You are one of the greatest teachers of our era. Even Socrates thinks you're one of a kind."

"Ah, shucks. Before we get involved in profound philosophical matters of truth, let me introduce to you my special assistant Onomatopoeia, his nickname is Snapcracklepop, or just Boomer for short. He travels with me far and wide and performs whatever tasks that I need to have done. He's very good at forcing non-payers to pay, he's a heavy and very dependable, in fact, he may be the very model of the perfect democratic man. He does exactly what he's told with no back lip and he's perfectly happy. He thinks that he can think but clearly he's mostly a dullard without a clue, things just spin in his head. It's all just a rush for him."

Boomer interrupts abruptly in a lisping nasal tone very similar to that of Alcibiades, "Yea, Boss here says dah I'm the best, you'no. I have an opinion dah on just about everything as long as you tell me what it is, you'no. If I could vote I would always vote with the majority, whatever they wanted. Neat, huh? I do whatever my Boss says. Cut taxes small government, that's my mantra. If I repeat it enough I'm sure it will be true, at least in my own mind. It sure feels right if nothing else. Once I chanted the prayer 'cut taxes small government' 5,000 times. It purges one of all thought and made me very popular, you'no. The truth is whatever you think it is that is the very most self-serving. I'm almost a philosopher like Boss here. Cool."

Parmenides smiles. "Isn't he cute? In his youth he played for the great sports team the Wackers. It was an odd game that they played and it was called Pigskin. The object of this game was rather straightforward and very entertaining, as eleven men lined up an either side and they let loose a greased pig, I mean a living, biting, shitting pig, about 40 pounds. The goal was for each team to fight over the pig and run to the end of the field where there was a hoplite spike and stick him to it. Of course the pig was not happy and squealed like Hades, but it was real funny and what a mess, always a real pile of poop. You got points for a stuck pig. But more points were scored by beating the crap out of your opponent. A stuck pig was worth one point but a broken skull was worth seven and broken bones three. The final score was usually something like 103 to 102. You can figure usually ten to twelve stuck pigs, just enough for dinner. Onomatopocia here was a hero at this game, breaking all records for head injuries and now he is my disciple. Of course Pigskin was an immensely popular spectator sport, really just one more excuse to get drunk and fornicate. As the eleven on each side went back and forth across the field, sticking one pig after another, the drunken crowd would roar in delight as one more round of drinks were inhaled. It was all such great fun and the only real cost was a morning headache and the realization that one had spent all of one's money and it was back to the poorhouse. To keep the masses in a perpetual state of stupor, the authorities often subsidized the next Pigskin match, becoming like a corporate sponsor. So Boomer here is a fine representation of that very happy time when all was as mindless as it was eternally predictable. He's ready, willing, and able to do anything I tell him but don't get too close, he bites. By the way, have you bought my latest book, my Magnum Anus, called *The Trouble with Youth is that it's Wasted on Socrates*. Kids today waste too much time listening to that old windbag when they could be doing something much more productive like playing Pigskin and making something of themselves, and the clones in that pickled fickled democratic Assembly ought to demand it. If more kids were like Boomer here we would have far fewer juvenile delinquents and more discipline for when they go into the army. Yes, it is discipline that we need, not interminable questions with no answers, comprende? Socrates is an unaffiliated free lance pseudo intellectual rabble rouser street walker pain in the keyster that makes me look bad and ought to be put out of business, if he had a business. He's wrecking it for the rest of us real intellectuals who need to get paid to make a comfortable living. The real purpose of philosophy is to get a job and eat well. That pighead makes us all look like a bunch of money grubbers. He's a very bad example. I spell this all out in greater detail in my book, I'm sure you will buy it."

Alcibiades is a little dismayed. "That's a little harsh on Socrates. My own experience with him is that he is the kindest, most considerate, most thoughtful, and most insightful person possible. He sometimes makes people look bad by comparison, but that's not his fault, and being so genuinely an upstanding example it easily reflects poorly upon the rest of us who are generally not so kind, much less considerate, without a clear thought in the head, and without a clue as to this or that. Such a supreme example is bad news to the rest of us by comparison, perhaps you included."

Parmenides erupts, "I'll be giggered, of all the audacity. For such a handsome young man talking like that will get you in trouble. Just believe whatever your elders tell you. I'm 137, listen carefully. Are you implying that I may be jealous of that gadflyified plug?"

"No, not at all, but I myself cannot live up to his standard of excellence but I hope to respect him for that, not slander him or bad mouth him like you. He makes me feel shame for all my bad deeds. His example doesn't help me much, and after the fact I'm not proud of myself in the least. It's none of his doing, but all my own. Enough of this. We need to tap into your special wisdom. We need to know how to form a secret society and then give it a name. Tell us all about naming."

Parmenides grumps. "That secret society is kind of easy. Don't tell anybody. But first I will tell you about the truth and then names. Some think that the truth is that all is one but in actual fact that's a bunch of hogwash and the truth is really that one is all. Brilliant, right, don't you think? I make a living saying that. By the way, an additional piece of truth is don't play leapfrog with a unicorn. That could cost you dearly. Another good one is don't use the word jack as a verb! That's some real paydirt. I charge for it every chance I get."

He points to Boomer. "Collect some money." Boomer growls as Alcibiades flips him a drachma.

Alcibiades is somewhat amazed. "That's it? Saying all is one or one is all is one and all the same to me. And you charge for that philosophical wisdom?"

"You betcha. I charge for everything even if nothing is learned. Kids today are mostly dimwits just like their parents. A fool and his money are soon parted. We philosophers have to eat too, and I like to eat a lot. Another way to get at the truth is to say that 'everything is nothing or nothing is everything.'"

"Well, moving on, we need help with naming our secret society. Tell us about names."

Parmenides expounds briskly. "For starters, when one is all, or all is one, I forget which, there is very little need for names, its all the same, but if you insist I can charge you, or I mean, help you with names. It's easy to make stuff up. Sometimes I get confused myself. But, of course, it's really quite easy as the truth is whatever I say it is. Who's to say otherwise? Perhaps Socrates, but he's an old crank and since he doesn't charge for his wisdom it has no value. Enough of this. Let's start with your name, Alcibiades."

Alcibiades is pleased. "Very good idea."

Parmenides continues. "Alcibiades is a Spartan word that means chameleon with huge member."

Alcibiades purrs. "Perfect. I like that part about the huge member and the chameleon. One always needs to change with necessity in order to get ahead and get what one wants."

Parmenides goes on. "Your friend here has an interesting name as well. Dyclyssides is a Minoan word that means gelding with attitude. Sometimes a neutered stud doesn't yet realize that he's nothing more than a plow horse and at anytime subject to the spit. When the next outrage requires sufficient celebration his destiny is a turn at the rotisserie, really just a piece of meat, attitude or no."

Alcibiades is amused. "Hey, Dyc, what do you think of that?"

Dyclyssides is not impressed. "I sure won't pay for that bit of philosophical wisdom. I can believe whatever I want to and nobody will convince me otherwise. The truth is whatever I want it to be, I'm that smart. If something is black and I say it's white, guess what, it's white and if you don't like it you can kiss my ass."

Parmenides quickly responds. "Whatever you think doesn't matter as these are the facts as fact, very factual, a virtual factoid-orama, get over it, be happy! And now for your next little friend. Rumshypocrites is a Persian word that means shorty with big mouth.

Alcibiades smirks. "Rummy, you happy with that? Do you prefer Rummy or just Hypocrite?"

Rumshypocrites, also not impressed, in a whining, sniveling voice speaks. "Gee, my mama told me my name means golden boy with big eyelashes."

"Your mommy was making stuff up," Alcibiades retorts, "as you were worthless from the beginning, she told me so. Enough of this. How about our little runt here, Georgiripides?"

Parmenides is tiring. "That's easy. It a royal Egyptian word from the old period that means asshole of a chicken."

Alcibiades is pleased. "Hey Georgie boy, that's kind of funny, isn't it?"

Georgiripides says with a grimaced smirk. "This guy's nuts. Wait till my daddy hears about this. He won't pay the fee for sure."

Parmenides quips. "The whiners that always need their mommy's tit and daddy's money, never pay, it's predictable. They all think they're entitled. Most of them couldn't stand up straight without a prod in the rear. Being born of privilege it is their privilege to be perfectly useless, parasites to one and all. And surely always remember, 'a bird in the hand is worth two in the bush.' Boomer works over this kind of special problem."

Alcibiades has had his fill of names. "Enough about personal names. I think you hurt Georgi's feelings, but now to other matters. We need a name for our new secret Society for Intervention Elsewhere. We want to promote wars elsewhere with other people's kids under the cover of patriotic gobblegook. What should we name this?"

Parmenides is intrigued. "I like that part about being secret and other people's kids. You need something short and sweet, a real pearl. How about Neocon?

Alcibiades impressed says. "Sounds good to me. What does it mean?"

Parmenides asserts. "It comes from an old bag of tricks and means Plan A set in stone, mindlessly. It also means to deceive others in a new way. It's what is called propaganda, when loving parents are convinced to give over their children to be slaughtered in the phantasy of profit for others. It's just a new way to make money at someone else's expense. There are a few costs though. The grieving parents are given a special commemorative coin minted for just this occasion of their son's death. That usually is enough to keep them quiet. Their grief is often too much to bother to complain. But something more can be said about this nefarious concept of Neocon. It is the orchestration of political slogans and propagandistic lies as a ruse for the imposition of overwhelming military power for the purpose of exercising political control and dominion over those who would hope otherwise, or the projecting of power where one has no business, simply because it feels good and reinforces all of one's self-serving, self-gratifying, and self-aggrandizing opinions of oneself, which have nothing to do with anything that would ever smack of reality. It's called the Pox Americanabacillus Docrtrine, and it is the straightest road to Hell."

"Perfect. What does all that mean? You're a genius."

Parmenides says in a wistful tone. "I don't know exactly what it means, but I know one thing and that is that it means casualties, lots of casualties, enough to inscribe the names of the dead on acres of black marble slabs. I heard Socrates once say that it's a form of insanity and that the only antidote is knowing thyself, acting in moderation and, most emphatically, minding one's own business. But enough of the dismal consequences of a failed Doctrine that is so well intended. Moving on, you now have a name appropriate to your new secret society intent upon inflicting terror. It's time to leave or, better yet, time to get paid. I have to carry my teaching forward to others to save the world from deception and themselves." Alcibiades gives him some coins and off the old duffer and Boomer go, rubbing the gold pieces together gleefully. Thus was born the Neocon secret society. It was a motley crew. The chameleon with huge member led the way as the gelding and big mouth played their lesser roles. But, in the end, daddy's money trumped and the famous O-ring of a chicken was led to believe that he was in charge, the decider, deciding once and for all. He may have thought himself the big man but he was just a little man, a puppet on a string, for the profit of others. No one ever had the heart to tell him the truth as it was painful to watch a grown child cry. Sadly, he had a great time. Other people's dead children just made it all that much more fun.

☆ ☆ ☆ ☆ ☆

At the height of his youthful popularity, when surely destined to stand tall in the democratic Assembly, leading Athens to victory wherever he could, Alcibiades had the eminent good fortune to participate in the games at Olympia in the Peloponnesus as an entry in the chariot races, in fact not one but seven races in all. This was an unprecedented level of participation as to enter even one chariot race required the wealth of a rich man. Alcibiades of course went for the max with money being no object. A massive entourage had accompanied him to this quadrennial event, tending to horses and the master, and everyone enroute made way for him as he traveled the fair distance from Athens to Olympia. It was a spectacle to behold and with such an ostentatious display of excess, the logical expectation was that Alcibiades would win and he intended not to disappoint anyone at all cost.

The Olympic Games presented all that was best in Greek culture. All conflict and hostility among city-states was interrupted as peace reigned throughout the land for the duration of the Games. But, just as in warfare, competition was keen as the only thing as good as killing an enemy in battle was besting him in athletic competition in front of thousands from everywhere. To win at the Games was to achieve an enduring fame that would be chiseled into stone as even the great sculptor Pheidias spent time at Olympia carving in marble the full statues of past victors. It was an extensive site dominated by the Temple to Apollo, placed at the center around which extended the Palestra where the man on man contests were held. Wrestling in the nude, smeared with olive oil, the combatants could find advantage only in the possession of skill, strength, and stamina. The vanquished would never have reason for complaint as all victory was fairly won. The fact of fair play was the hallmark of Olympic competition. No one had ever violated this solemn and religious pledge. The complex also included housing for athletes and staff, treasuries, shrines, and most famously, a running track which one entered through an arched tunnel way. The finish line was inlaid marble and marked the point of infinite exultation. Crossing the line ahead one could virtually be immediately ascended into heaven. To the victor went all the acclaim as no one ever would bother to remember the second place finisher. Nothing could come of an effort that was but a fractional second late. Further extending around the running track was the chariot course where the riches required for entry made it the most anticipated event of all.

Into this sacred domain entered Alcibiades with absolutely no intention of losing.

Sampson and Solomon were an exquisite example of horseflesh. This team of half-brothers was Alcibiades' best chance at victory but the competition would be steep. The Spartan Lysander had the team of David and Goliath who possessed that same stately pose of strength and courage. By no means would an Alcibiadean victory be guaranteed from the start with this experienced pair ready, willing, and able to do battle. Something would need to be done in order to ensure a Spartan defeat at the hands of our Athenian Atlas. Cheating had never even been considered but that was before the onslaught of Alcibiades, the most handsome man in all of Greece.

Being confident of easy victory in the qualifying races, Alcibiades saved his disturbia for the final race against Lysander. The two teams would battle it out as the final event of the Games when the lull of peace would then give way to the realities of renewed war. The political situation was unhappy all around and victory for Alcibiades would bode well for the Athenian cause. Much was at stake in this battle of charioteers. Since security was tight there would be no chance to get at the Spartan horses overnight so as to inflict some sort of damage. Any misdeed would need to be done during the race. Alcibiades needed to use his imagination. He had a good luck charm that was a rather shinny piece of mirror that he wore around his neck. It was always fun to look at himself. It reflected sunlight into a concentration that could very easily spook a horse. Administered at the right time this light beam could blind and disorient. The plan was quite simple. At the start of the race, Georgiripides, the asshole of a chicken, would reflect the light into the eyes of Goliath and hopefully create enough spook and panic to hinder the start, giving Alcibiades ample time to roll ahead to the finish line. The malefactor positioned himself to the side as everyone looked another way and with the chaos of the start of the race, no one noticed the misdeed. The focused sunbeam mixed with the glitter of the spectacle itself and nothing was clearly seen. The ploy worked to perfection and Alcibiades easily won. The blinded horse went nuts, forcing his team mate off to the side and once they achieved full speed they crashed into the spectator benching, killing five. The horses were destroyed, Alcibiades won by default, but Lysander was pissed. He knew something had been done as these horses never faulted a start, but what? He didn't know. When Alcibiades was celebrating victory with his entourage he caught the glance of Lysander and then understood the look of death. Of course it didn't faze him in the least, or so he thought. He just may encounter that singular look again, odds were good. In his mind, lying and cheating were perfectly fair ways to achieve success in a world that honored only winners. If unintended consequences were to cause collateral damage, that was so much the better as it buffed up the drama. The dead spectators ought to have felt privileged to die such a grisly death in the glorification of Alcibiades, the highest representation of the beautiful people, which surely was of course their designated role in life as the common masses must serve the needs of the uncommon few, the rich and famous. The natural way of the world was perfectly affirmed once again, Alcibiades smiled to himself, satisfaction consummated. Similarly, the collateral damage in war ought to have found the same lesson as the many innocent dead are but the plaything of those who are in it only for themselves. There are no such innocents, all must suffer what they must. His only real concern was the unreliability of Georgiripides who would surely talk but there were ways to shout him into a humiliation that would lend little creditability to any of his babblings about reflected light.

The magnificent pair of chariot horses became flesh and were spitted on a barbecue rotisserie, the sauce was excellent, that would feed the full entourage of the victor but Lysander was without appetite, stewing in his rage, already relishing the day sometime soon that he would cross paths with this cheat and impostor, confident that when final comeuppance would be delivered true amends would be made and a feast of justice served. The gods themselves would not allow such an audacious fraud to win the final garland of victory and disgrace the spirit of fair play and sportsmanship. The pretty boy was destined for a bitter demise. Lysander could wait.

The following year would find a haranguing Alcibiades before the democratic Assembly trying to convince the easily convinced that there is good cause for preventive war in Sicily. In support of his claim to leadership he affirms the glory of his Olympic victory in the chariot race against the hated Spartan Lysander. Without conscience or moral self-awareness, driven only by a blazing ambition, Alcibiades plunges forward with a strategy which will be the single most decisive reason for the final Athenian defeat. Rumor and innuendo though are rife but it is still too early to undercut the charming pretty boy as the Athenians vote to expand the war, choosing aggression and then consequently achieving losses beyond all comprehension. For now though they will follow their Olympic champion. Lysander may have much to say in the end, indeed.

☆ ☆ ☆ ☆ ☆

The protracted Civil War that pitted Greek against Greek, Spartan against Athenian, engulfed many seemingly innocent non-combatants. Each side marshaled its alliances with numerous cities and islands but some few trusted in the sanctity of neutrality. Not caring a wit which side prevailed over the other, these neutral and out of the way places felt safe in their non-belligerence. One such place was the island of Melos. As each side had assured itself of an easy and quick victory, it is now 15 years into the conflict and measures of desperation are beginning to look normal. Alcibiades, as an Athenian commander, proposes the subjugation of the Melians. Their presumptive neutrality could not be trusted and as the rigor of domestic discipline tightened, it became necessary to enforce compliance everywhere. The Melians themselves were in the wrong place at the wrong time and Alcibiades meant to teach them a very hard lesson. It would be rather easy. With his three associates, Dyclyssides, Rumshypocrites, and Georgiripides, he sails south at the head of a fleet of warships sufficient for the job ahead. Upon arrival, his triremes are idled at oar, as he offloads onto a smaller skiff and is rowed to shore. An array of similar craft provides conveyance for hoplite soldiers needed as a show of force. Since too few men have come ashore for any kind of attack, the Melian leadership meets the contingent of Athenians in front of their walls. They naturally despise these bullies, as past experience has not been good, but the fact of the warships menaces and the Melians are visibly distressed.

"We have come from the city of Athens with news for you," Alcibiades proclaims. "I am a representative with full powers to execute the will of my people of the democratic Assembly. We wish you well and that you take our decision to heart. But time is short, so I will be most direct. Simply, we are at war with the Spartans. You are unfortunate from our point of view in two ways. You are a colony of Sparta and your island sits in the middle of our sphere, the Aegean is an Athenian domain. Your neutrality is meaningless to us. We therefore have decided that this cannot continue."

The Melian leader is dismayed and startled. "Wait, wait, not so fast, before you get yourself in a fighting lather. Yes, we are a colony of Sparta but we are neutral in this war that you two have brought upon yourselves. We want no part of it and mean no harm to anyone. We will live in peace with everyone!"

Alcibiades interrupts and quickly asserts. "Wait yourself. Please shut up. We are not here to discuss this issue; we are here to settle it as we please. The merit of this case in your minds is not a concern of the Athenian Assembly. We are at war with Spartan terrorists and all measures must be imposed that aid in this battle for our freedom. You need to be taught the first lesson of power. The strong do what they can and the weak suffer what they must." (5.89)

The Melian leader stammers, "But, but…"

Alcibiades lifts his hand to quiet his opponent. "Again, please shut up. We are not here to negotiate. Might makes right. We are here to be done with you Melians once and for all. Frankly, you're a bad example. Others in our Empire see your neutrality and think that maybe that would be good for themselves. People with opinions all their own are the first sign of trouble. The next thing they vote to quit paying us for the privilege that we extend to them of paying us and we then have to send a costly force to return them to their senses before they had this new opinion. During this bigger war with Sparta, this doesn't work so well. So here it is. You are now part of the Athenian Empire, the greatest democracy in the world, and you will quit any dealings with those fanatical Spartans, and you will start paying us now." Georgiripides steps forward and hands Alcibiades a scroll and Alcibiades points to him to hand it to the Melians. Alcibiades continues, "This document, voted upon and approved by the Athenian democracy, tells you what you now owe us. 20% of all goods of the field will be collected and shipped to Athens at the conclusion of the harvest. You also must build and man 10 triremes a year for service in the Athenian navy."

"What, are you nuts?"

Alcibiades calmly responds, "No, we are at war."

"That's impossible! We can't afford that. It's not right. Who the blue blazes do you think you are? We will fight!"

Alcibiades turns and gestures towards his warships and sighs, his lisp no longer endearing. "Well and good. It is your choice. You have 24 hours to see the obvious. Capitulate to us or die. It is that simple and absolutely inevitable. You have no choice in this, end of matter. The Athenian democracy has decided for you." The Athenians turn and walk back to their boat. The Melians erupt into turmoil, talking all at once and shaking their fists and shouting curses. The first Melian raises a hand for silence.

"We will fight these democratic bastards, these arrogant bullies, and Sparta will come to our aid and save us. It's not right. Let us vote now. All in favor of defense of the homeland." There is a great clamor and all hands are raised as they go behind the walls of their city.

As predicted by Alcibiades, the battle ensues and Melos falls. He stands before the defeated in full battle armor, holding in hand a decree. Defeated and bedraggled Melians dejectedly listen. "Using very poor judgment, that I personally advised you against, you Melians have fought the wrong fight and have lost and now must pay dearly. You could have saved yourselves but no, you chose to be brave and stupid, well that is over and so is each of you. The Athenian Assembly now stipulates." He unrolls the scroll. "All Melian men will be put to death and all women and children sold into slavery at the slave markets of Athens." He rolls the scroll and then adds. "I myself will take the most beautiful teenage girl for my own use on the voyage home. Soldiers please begin the execution of this order of the Athenian people." A long line of men are forced into position as they are moved to the foot of the city wall and the individual executions begin, a slash to the throat usually effective, and then a push into a ditch. As Alcibiades walks away he mutters to his companions. "Someone ought to figure out a way to kill a lot of people quickly, all at once, and from a distance, it's just too messy up close. I'll have to put some of those new natural scientists to work on that, it would be interesting theoretical work for them. Perhaps something from the sky. We could rain down death upon anyone, anywhere, without them ever suspecting a thing. They would be dead before they knew they were dying. It would be beautiful, simply beautiful." Slaughter continues as they return to their ship.

This was arguably the cruelest and most brutal act of this long civil war, although not without precedence, as such an order had been executed before by others against still others. The Athenians acted in their self-interest with a complete disregard for the natural rights of others. Their position of power assured them that this was their perfect right to which others must naturally defer. But the brutality was beyond all proportion, as all the men were killed, and women and children sold. If there are gods they surely would have been watching. But the cycle of history turns, and it would perhaps be possible that this slaughter be re-visited, as others too find themselves on the receiving end. Time will tell.

The Spartans had their own story of atrocity to justify. The Helots were the target, their servant class. A deceptive ploy stretches the imagination's ability to comprehend the sheer incomprehensibility of this act. Surprisingly, Helots had fought on behalf of the Spartans with honor, dignity, and distinction, fighting bravely to the end, as need be. The Spartans sent word to these souls that the bravest of them all should come forward and be acknowledged and celebrated by the Spartan elites. A total of 2000 unsuspecting warriors stepped forward to receive their reward. Congratulations and well-wishing were made all around until the Spartans on the sly killed all 2000 compatriots. The presumptive reasoning was that such confident and capable fighters would be an internal threat to Sparta and the best policy would be to preventively do them in to save any possible further trouble. A mass grave became the final reward for honorable service.

The sobering truth is that the Athenian annihilation of Melos and the Spartan killing of deceived Helots was not the exceptional case at all but rather the established standard operating procedure, now the accepted methodology in a war to the last man. Many other examples of atrocity reach to this same level of perfection, compounding the horror to an even greater degree of magnitude. The length of the Peloponnesian War created the context for this move to more and more vicious acts of violence. A critical fact is that it was not the commanding general's decision as to the life or death of those captured, rather it was the vote of the democratic Assembly in Athens that dictated such terms. As the people at home suffered so would everybody else. Generals were often punished in due course for any perceived instances of inexcusably lenient behavior. Of course, once utter brutality established itself as the norm, there could be only more of the same as a tradition of sorts simply perpetuated itself. Nothing could alter a logic of reprisal that with each turn offered renewed opportunities. Cold calculation and disembodied military logic allow men to justify acts of brutality that are beyond any sense of possibility. Such acts of the final solution are as common as wars are inevitable.

☆ ☆ ☆ ☆ ☆

Being at the hub of Greek commerce and wealth, Athens was the epicenter of a network of dramatic cultural accomplishments. It attracted anyone with a notion about anything. Mostly these crackpots and wiseacres came from nearby, within the domain where the Greek language was understood, but one day the oddest fellow of all arrived from afar of a very dark complexion and the wildest hair imaginable. He said that he had come from a land beyond the eastern boundary of the kingdom of Persia, nearly as far as the far side of the moon, a distance so vast that no one believed him but his personality was so pleasant and engaging that we all loved him, in an manner of speaking. He called himself Siddhartha. He had walked this great distance in the company of a Greek speaking goatherd named Yogurtus and on the way had sufficient time to learn a little of our perfect language. He spoke in fits and starts but was surprisingly understandable as his wealth of hand gestures sufficiently supplemented his truncated vocabulary and, with a little prodding and pulling, a mutual understanding of sorts was both possible and rewarding. He was the most interested in our religious and philosophical beliefs, but the spectacle of the recently completed Parthenon was an ever amazing wonder to him. Only truly all-powerful gods could have done something so divine. He would stare in disbelief. Some days he would just touch it, holding his hand upon a pillar, entranced, reconfirming its fact, then shaking his head. He could never get enough of it.

Siddhartha's overwhelming fascination with the Parthenon set Socrates to thinking anew about this most famous military weapon, this projection of power, which convinced so many others of the Empire of the good sense of submission to the Athenian will. Clearly, architecturally, it was a masterpiece but in such a way that something insightful could perhaps be said of human reality itself. Sitting upon the elevated outcropping that is the Acropolis, it was already sited in such a way as to point heavenward. The vertical linear upsurge of the columns sent the eye on a line to the zenith, something comprehended mentally as the spiritual move upwards towards ideality, to an essential being of things that is without any material encumbrance yet, at the same time, the eye can choose to reverse the line of sight to the nadir, downward. Mirroring the upsurge of the columns is the downward plunge of the eye to the base, to the foundation, that is perfectly planted upon the earth. If ideality leads the eye upward, then material reality leads the eye downward and, within the nexus of the two, there is constituted a tension of equipoise that perfectly binds the two together. Flying upward and plunging downward, a stasis of force is consummated, a gripping together of opposites, which is perhaps the consummate ideal of human existence itself. Intrinsically opposing forces achieve a permanent place in the non-movement of the stone of the earth, perfectly aligned. A balance is achieved that engages the imagination in the experience of the mentality of ideality with the materiality of reality, and this then being the being of the human being as a full participant in the drama of life and history. The tension of tragedy and comedy, as forming the reality of self-consciousness, is again invoked as the quintessential achievement of being human. The witnessing of the force and presence of the monolithic Parthenon is a religious experience that elevates while anchoring human consciousness in an exultation that is without *hubris*. It reaches forward yet is set into place, it minds its own business, as it were, and, accordingly, inspires one to a greater comprehension of oneself. Simply, the Parthenon is, at the same time, a Temple to Athena, a religious shrine, and a Treasury of the State, a worldly bank, the perfect sharing of the ethereal and the real. An interesting psychological tendency is possible where one narrowly sees but one or the other but not both, to understand it as either a Temple or a Treasury as one's attitude is dominated by the one direction or the other. The superlative experience is to comprehend this fabulous structure as representing both tendencies simultaneously. It is the movement from the divine to the human, god and man, back and forth, as depicted in stone, a most profound revelation indeed. In some quarters this movement back and forth would be the essential definition of love, the reconciliation of being and nothingness, the West and the East, Socrates and Siddhartha, all there for one to see if one were so inclined to choose. It was no wonder that Siddhartha was captivated as nothing could be more.

Needless to say and understandably perfect, Siddhartha and Socrates were a hit. For the first time Socrates had met his match. Usually Socrates had someone tied in knots after one, sometimes two questions. If anyone ever got a third question they were so mad at Socrates for showing them their natural ignorance that they would stomp off in a huff. No such capitulation from Siddhartha. His perfect advantage was that he knew nothing except that he knew a little something about that nothing. Apparently nothing is something. Only a couple of rustics like these two knuckleheads could make something of nothing with a straight face. Of course the rest of us never knew if it was all just a big joke, some sort of ironic inside laugh. They talked and talked interminably about this nothing and we were all sure not to interrupt as nothing good could possibly come of that. We were all hoping too that perhaps this Siddhartha would be good for Socrates and get him back to being a normal human being like the rest of us. Xantippe, his wife, often complained about his poor breadwinning skills and they seldom had any bacon.

But her wishes were not to be fulfilled as the two talkers talked and then talked some more. They were left alone but bits and pieces were heard here and there that made perfectly no sense to anyone. It was embarrassing.

Apparently, this man from the East had an entirely different view than that of our Western perspective. A brief summary is painfully difficult to piece together. A comparison of views hinged upon the nature of the ego and that ego's desire. Is the ego to be full or empty, active or passive, caring or not? The principle of "knowing thyself" posits the ego as a full, active, and caring reality. It reaches out into the world in an attitude of creation and constitution. It wants to do and to build a world for the greater satisfaction of all. It pushes beyond temporary limitations in order to know and to know systematically, which means to know scientifically. This active fullness powers an impetus that will transform the material and mental well being of the world through the possibility of abundant production. Desires of sundry appeal will find gratification here. When all of this works in a natural harmony there will be expressed the Idea of the Good in its highest manifestation, when idea meets world and a reality is constituted that encompasses all. The way to this technological and spiritual paradise though is fraught with difficulty as an ideal trajectory is subject to the gravity of egotistical greed. The ego can do wonderful things but when full of itself equally horrible things. At any and every point along the way there will be required a choice one way or another. It is the odyssey of the Western spirit to actively participate in the ever transforming power of the constituting ego. The odyssey of the Eastern spirit is no odyssey at all but rather an imposition of an oppressive weight upon any such constituting ego and instead what is left is the institution of a permanent nothingness of that ego.

With such a reversal is introduced the opacity of Siddhartha's view. Empty and passive, the ego is without desire, and without desire there can be no cares to torment the person in a series of predictable failures. In desiring nothing the bliss of nothingness is transformed in the redemption of the eternal recurrence of the same. Living on virtually nothing, there can be no possible abundance, as a passive compliance with the conditions of the force of immediate circumstances necessitates a world without change. The ego will have found nothing to care about as desires are non-existent in the final confirmation of a pure nothingness.

From the respective perspectives of the East and the West, the other appears to be meaningless and without merit. Socrates and Siddhartha had each made the case for the one and then the other and an impasse loomed that risked the possibility that they would quit talking. Then one day the most amazing thing happened. A spaceship landed. You can imagine our surprise.

It had been a crystal clear day but was now in the twilight zone before night. The two philosophical pugilists were sitting a distance from the city, among the birds and the bees, nearly spent from a day of talking when there was this whirligig sound that seemed to come from everywhere. The twilight then reflected off a metallic surface and lights flashed in synchronized fashion, as an immense round object descended to the ground and came in for a landing. Once aground the sound subsided and then there was nothing for awhile. Finally, breaking the unbearable suspense, a panel of some sort retracted and an opening appeared and promptly three short guys stepped out from the spaceship. They were really short with big eyes and nothing by the way of facial expression. They looked around and descended a short ramp that had been miraculously extended and then there they stood directly upon Greek soil. It was something to behold. Thousands of people had quickly gathered upon our walls with a clear but distant view. It was close enough for most of us. At first it was natural to think that they were alien extraterrestrials, weird beings from a distant galaxy, because their vehicle was so otherworldly but they were from a distant land mass called Hudsonia, whatever that was, they didn't say, come for a visit. Siddhartha had already beshit himself in fright but Socrates confidently stepped forth and offered a greeting of welcome, anticipating a conversation like none other. They were configured as we humans but they looked preternaturally young, youthful but wise, perhaps aged without ill effects. Their stark baldness enhanced their ageless aspect. One stepped ahead of the others, the clear leader, and spoke with Socrates.

"Hello fellow earthlings, we Hudsonians have come in peace, without malice or evil intent. My name is Principia Universalis the 256th. We live in perfect harmony on our island and have noticed your consistent failure to achieve anything but serial warfare. We have come to help, to work through with you your marked propensity to end all disputes with warfare that then reduces to misery and annihilation all around. Very unfortunate indeed."

Socrates takes a deep breath and responds. "Eternal welcome to our precious rock in the Aegean. Indeed, we are troubled by war and can only imagine more of the same. Your help would be greatly appreciated."

"Due to a technological superiority we are able to listen in on any discussion you may have. We have been eavesdropping for years on the comings and goings of your rather pathetic lives to both our infinite amusement and perplexing chagrin. We know that you could do better. You are your own worst enemy. Your conflicts are all self-inflicted. You live in a state of primitive chaos."

Socrates look to the ground. "Very well said. Please continue."

"We need to retire for awhile now and will reappear tomorrow. We need to make some technical adjustments to our inverse-ratio-jet-propulsion-anti-matter-laser-beam-rockets. It's just precautionary. I hope you understand." With that the three turned and quickly returned to their spaceship. The ramp retracted, the door closed, and off they went, ascending slowly and then, in a moment, accelerating directly away.

Socrates turns to Siddhartha. "Are you OK? What's that stinkatude?"

"Bejesus Socrates, I beturded myself and you instead calmly step toward these aliens as if Mr. Universalis is you best friend. How do you do it? Weren't you afraid?"

"Assuming that everyone, including someone from afar, is your best friend is a good start. The benefit of the doubt is the first step towards mutual respect and understanding. What could be more than meeting these guests as equals? What is there to be afraid of? If they wanted to destroy us, they would, but they didn't. So let's talk with them. Bedeucing oneself is just bad manners and not the best way to start a conversation."

"OK Socrates, you win." The two returned to the city, Siddhartha chattering and Socrates thinking. The spectator crowd broke up and everyone was abuzz about the Hudsonians' return visit. It would be momentous. Without further ado, they appeared the next day as promised and resumed a conversation with the ever alert Socrates and the humanely cleansed Siddhartha.

All occurred as before and Universalis spoke first. "It may look to be that we are meddling in your affairs but we only intend to advise and leave you to your own choices. Your failures have come to be so perfectly predictable that we thought some perspective would be useful. We once had the same problem. We have monitored your conversation regarding the West and the East, the ego and the non-ego, the active and the passive, and found both views essentially lacking the reality of the other. It's a matter of balance, of the harmony of ego and non-ego, of the active and the passive. When this harmonic balance is achieved the ego finds a humility that opens new spectrums of reality. When the ego achieves, when it constitutes an objective reality, it is easily prone to choosing an attitude that affirms an exaggeration of itself. Simply, it descends into an attitude of "being full of itself." That my friend is your problem, the interminable running about that serves only the lone ego at the expense of something greater. The most immediate form of being full of oneself is the minding of someone else's business in the hopes of getting something for nothing. It is the making war in order to secure to oneself the rightful goods of others. It is the imposition of force that serves only to further one's own self-aggrandizement. It is the living beyond one's means and then extracting from others the shortfall. And, finally, it is the being perfectly stupid in an arrogance that is consummately without any notion of humility. The ego is potentially a powerful agent of achievement but without the balance of respect for the greatest good it becomes a weapon capable of infinite destruction."

Siddhartha needed to speak, he had never listened so long before in his life. "I beg your pardon Universalis but isn't that my point exactly, the power of the East. Destroy the ego and live happily ever after. Remain within the limits of nothingness and there will be no ego to busybody the world into destruction. From nothingness nothing can arise except that special something that keeps us without desire of any sort."

"You are essentially only partially right. Without the ego there is nothing but the eternal recurrence of the same, the ever repetition of the mindlessly opaque. To be human requires more. The active ego is the beacon of light that enlightens the reality of self-consciousness, it clears the way to the project of "knowing thyself" that adds eternal value to the being of being human. In the context of ego, of empowered thinking, constitution, and achievement, there is found the harmony that is the end of war and the beginning of a universal friendship that knows no limits to personal happiness." This was an amazing piece of wisdom indeed. Both Socrates and Siddhartha nodded accent, each lost to his own thinking, the one thinking of the idea of harmony from the perspective of the ego and the other thinking the same from the perspective of nothingness.

Universalis resumed his speech. "We Hudsonians were once like you are now, lost to a confusion of self-inflicted destruction. I am the 256th leader in a line that began with the demise of a crackpot tyrant that had no sense of restraint and instead rode an overwhelming attitude of arrogance that almost brought us to an end. We saved ourselves just in time. His name was

Bushwacker the Second. He had all the symptoms, arrogant, full of himself, presumptuous, and without conscience. He got us into wars without end for the benefit of his band of similar idiots but the rest of us were the real fools for abdicating our responsibility and then thinking that the little dictator would make things easier for the rest. The idea of easy profits trumped living within our means and we were on the road to Hell. Just in time we came to our senses and have made restitution to all those who we had harmed. It's an ancient history to us now but every new generation relives the lessons of the perils of fat egos and the allure of getting something for nothing. Socrates, there is little more to add. Perhaps this can be of some use in salvaging the Greeks from themselves. Start with Alcibiades. Another thing, something that you will find difficult to comprehend as you live at such a primitive level of existence. Technological development extends into infinite levels of expertise. Once we quit spending so much on our over extended military, we were able instead to invest in scientific and technological advancement. The results simply stagger the imagination and were perfectly dazzling. We developed, after extensive time and investment, a power source, an engine, that produces energy at a stupendous level of efficiency, out of nothing. This engine is able to absorb ambient static electricity and convert it into a power source sufficient to travel millions of miles in perfect ease. Of course our spaceship is the result. We found that once we quit killing our neighbors with very expensive weapons it was infinitely more satisfying to become friends with all the universe. We broke the religious cycle of needing and then nurturing an enemy, a perpetual Cold War, as it were, of needing to divide the world into two, the good and the bad, with us of course being the all too good, and consigning our children and grandchildren to ever more lethal levels of destruction, for no particular reason." With that he returned to his spaceship and was gone.

Siddhartha is astounded. "Well, Socrates, what do you make of all that? What do you think ambient static electricity is?"

"I suppose it may have something to do with the lightning bolts of Zeus, but who knows? Being as primitive as we are, I didn't have the heart to ask. But it's all very intriguing. What is the nature of the Hudsonians' technological advantage such that they would come here on a humanitarian mission? In being very clever with things, they must have come to a greater understanding of themselves. Somehow they created a technological mastery that came to serve the greater good. Usually advantage goes to the stronger who then uses it to consolidate that advantage to the natural chagrin of most others. They must have achieved an emotional, intellectual, and spiritual balance that constitutes a material and mental abundance that serves everyone. At its most primitive, technological excellence is sunk into military prowess which sooner or later will be consumed of itself. The magic of their stupendous travel indicates that they have not gravitated to this but have achieved a much higher level of utilization. Foregoing the false allure of military preponderance, they achieved instead a social and political balance that served them infinitely better. The cost of even a single trireme warship, which we build by the hundreds, undercuts any possibility of putting our technological wealth to work in any lasting and constructive way. Military spending is an attraction that ultimately achieves very little indeed. The Hudsonians must have learned to marshal their technological good fortune to the greater social good, allowing them to do such a spectacle thing as travel here."

This at least was the surmise of Socrates. Using the imagination it was theoretically possible to construct the beginning outline of reality. Whether true or not it was left until further notice when the specifics could be re-visited and greater evidence and judgment brought to bear. This concluded the talking of Socrates and Siddhartha. The man from the east intended to move further to the west as he had heard that at a place called Rome there may be potential disciples ready to listen to what he had to say about nothing. He had learned much from our Athenian gadfly but he was as much a walker as a talker and the dusty road beckoned.

Bidding adieu, he left, leaving us much to think about as, while we preached a philosophy of moderation, the balance and harmony of the east was as alien to us as excess was our natural element.

With the passage of time Socrates had other things to say about technology and matters military. Here is a patched together reading of his thoughts. An exaggerated emphasis on military spending as a presumption of security often times instead facilitates a bewitchingly odd reversal, wherein there is not more but less security. A self-fulfilling prophecy of sorts ensues. Our get-something-for-nothing foreign policy as the center of the Athenian Empire creates among those aligned an attitude of fear and loathing, as well as many minor ways in which to undercut our predominance. Our great military expenditures can often be neutralized by pinprick underbelly insurgencies where we least expect it and therefore least able to defend. What we lose with our policy of Empire is positive cooperation. Our many dependencies feel put upon in the manner of heavy taxation and exorbitant contributions to our fleet. They are forced to contribute to their own subjugation. Resentment resounds and we have to spend even more to compensate. This spiral of costs does not make us stronger and more secure but the very opposite, weaker and less secure.

The core problem though with the possession of an invincible military is that we then want to use it far in advance of its absolute necessity. Not mimicking the Spartans, who ever so reluctantly engage an enemy, we, on the other hand, are quickly willing to launch an attack when a compromised resolution was still possible. Once the killing begins our problems and costs accelerate astronomically. A big military can easily achieve an early advantage but often ever so quickly that edge is lost and the interminable battle of attrition gains traction. If victory is not quick the fight for the long haul can be long, very long. Big empires can be brought down simply when they presume for themselves so overwhelming a material advantage, that their slow moving sloth can be engulfed by things smaller and quicker. Our victory against the Persians 50 years ago attests to this fact. It was inconceivable to King Xerxes that he could lose, possessing such a vast assemblage, and yet in the end he not only lost but was routed in an annihilation that still humiliates the proud Persians. List them too as our absolute enemy.

Had we not built up such a vast fleet, had we more judiciously negotiated with our allies, had we chosen not to extract something-for-nothing, this war with Sparta would not have begun. If we had sought to cooperate rather than compete perhaps we could have done ever so much better. True security is not winning at war but rather cooperating in peace. It is the minding of one's own business and respecting others in doing the same.

☆ ☆ ☆ ☆ ☆

Little removed from the allied victories against Persia, two future giants of the Greek Classical era were born in the same year, sharing a birthright that encouraged sympathy and respect, Socrates and Nicias. Each played a role in the long battle with Sparta, as one died at the hands of the enemy and the other by the verdict of his fellow citizens. Throughout the years they had had occasion to exchange a few words, whether it be in the army or near the Acropolis and Agora. If Socrates was eminently self-confident then Nicias was perfectly timid. While the one sought through focused reflection the answers to human questions, the other reverted to prayer and expensive religious displays in order to think not at all about those questions. But, being a man of substance, utilizing the wealth of vast silver mines, Nicias was drawn into the public arena and achieved the status of an elected general. Socrates, on the other hand, being a man of poverty, stayed clear of the public arena and found a disdain and ridicule from many fellow citizens. One day, during the tumult over the projected military operation in Sicily, the two men met on the steps of the Temple of Hephaestus that overlooks the Agora.

Across the way sat the immense geological outcropping that is the Acropolis, upon which stood the ever resplendent Parthenon. Accompanying Nicias that day was a rather slight 12 year old neighbor boy by the name of Plato. The boy's parents were somewhat at a loss to know what to do with the child. He played poorly with the neighbor boys and just didn't fit in well, having been rather weird from the beginning, but he had an uncanny aptitude for language. He had learned to read and write nearly on his own and earlier than any of his peers and was obviously a distinctly intellectual cut above. Nicias had taken a liking to the boy and thought that his influence might perhaps be of some benefit to the child prodigy. One interesting trait of the boy was that he was an intent listener. Saying very little himself, his eyes showed a focus of possible understanding that often left attendant adults dismayed. Plato's serious intensity unnerved those around him but Nicias found him to be an intriguing companion, without a hint of any congressional relations that was so common with others. Plato tagged along and seemed to be the better for it. People sometimes referred to this child beyond his years as the Little Big Man.

Today's meeting with Socrates was unintended but the two aging acquaintances would always have time for each other. On the top step of the Temple Socrates sat and looked across the way, while Nicias sat to his right a step lower, and still lower sat Plato, looking up to the famed Socrates, on the verge of stammering something he knew not what.

"Very nice to see you Socrates."

"Well, Nicias, it has been awhile since we last talked but with the turmoil and chaos over the Sicily operation, I've thought about you often. I deeply respect your reserve and efforts to quell this surge to destruction that so many are intent upon."

"It just doesn't make any sense," continued Nicias, "for us to charge into a distant fight when our real enemies are so much closer to home. The cost and potential danger is astronomically greater than any possible gain. But that Alcibiades is an agitator like no other and so many are led by the nose by his good looks and smirky way of talking. He makes it all sound so good and profitable but, baby, it ain't."

"I couldn't agree more. He's got an irresistible charm but time will catch up with him and things may not transpire as he would have us all believe."

Nicias sighs deeply. "How did we get into this fix? How did things turn out so poorly?"

Socrates pauses, glancing to the activity of the Agora, perhaps inspired by the grandeur of the Acropolis and then begins. "Our world is of our own making. We all make little choices, here and there, that add up to big facts. We pursue our own self-interest with a complete disregard as to any impact upon others. We pride ourselves upon being who we are with no regard to the pride of others. We think ourselves bigger than life and are surprised when others disagree. Our relative success as a city convinces us of our absolute invincibility as an Empire."

Nicias is downcast. "In other words, you are saying that we as a city suffer from hubris, that crippling arrogance that dooms us to failure as if the gods themselves intended it to be so."

"Yes, hubris surely, but the gods have nothing to do with this. Good, bad, or ugly, we like to blame the gods for our activities but it is perfectly true that we constitute our own failure. We do it to ourselves. Even though first causes may be in a distant past, with each new decision, we take those causes as our own, reanimating them for our own purposes. When things go poorly we like to blame those causes but finally it is our own responsibility. Blaming something else is the first indicator that we truly know our own complicity but are too weak to acknowledge this glaring truth. We will surely take the credit for any success and as surely give the blame for any failure. That, of course, is why our failures easily escalate into an even greater disaster. In not recognizing our own responsibility, the ship of state is left adrift, so to speak, without any further guidance and that quickly hits the ever ready hidden reefs of calamity. We build, and equally, we unbuild."

Plato is mesmerized by the tone of the discussion. He doesn't fully understand but he knows he wants to. It is as if there is a click in the brain, a brilliant moment of insight that reveals to him the future direction of his life. Nothing could be more than this level of abstraction that trades in such terms as first causes, responsibility, and hubris, and he, Plato, will do what he can to think more clearly about such thing and that is his resolve today. Socrates becomes to him like a god, a fully resplendent being of a higher dimension of excellence, the idea of which will guide him all the days of his life. This could only be a glimmer, a hunch, a partial expectation, but from this day forward he would think like a man.

Nicias continues the discussion. "Is there an alternative?"

"Certainly, in a word, courage."

"But what is courage?"

"Courage is the resolve to remain within the limits of the possible. It is the clear headed knowing of the possible, or the effort to think without bias. It is the affirmation of the general interest over against the narrow-mindedness of passionate self-interest. The twin directives of minding one's own business and knowing thyself set the parameters for this resolve. Stated otherwise, courage is the resolve to remain a questioner and never to have thought oneself to have found a final answer that will then be set into ideological stone. Questioning entails a humility that shields one from the arrogance of hubris and allows one to remain open to yet more questioning. It is a question of seeking the truth while yet realizing that there will be no final answers as the very process of thinking must remain good until further notice. When further questioning is undercut by the lethargy of ideology, when slogans and spin replace clear thinking, then the way to unbuilding will loom large. Nothing is left to save us once the rigors of ideology exhaust any impetus to renewed thought. The demagogues and tyrants, the fast talkers without a clue, can now rule the roost as any kind of evil misdeed is permitted. Full of himself, full of failed ideas evermore, full of unholy expectation, full of crap, the downward road to perdition becomes slicker and slicker. The man of courage is he who stands up against this and says No, knowing that he will be trampled underfoot by the mob of idiots that think themselves to have found the Holy Grail of happiness in the misery that they are now intent upon inflicting upon others. And then, of course, when all ends in destruction, if that man of courage ought to miraculously have survived, he will be the first to be put to death to cover those truly responsible. Thinking, indeed, is a serious business, a deadly thing."

"With all of this heartache in our world, is there such a thing as happiness?"

"Happiness is a rather unfortunate thing. It suffers from a complete misunderstanding, very similar to its partner in confusion, love. The logical and natural tendency is to assume that happiness is a sort of objective acquisition, whether that be wealth, fame, domestic bliss, and those sorts of things. It is thought to be something that we procure and with that of course it can be unprocured, nullified, taken away. We teeter between happiness and unhappiness as the fortunes of fate oscillate one way or the other. But, remarkably, happiness is not a thing of possession but rather a simple choice. It is the choice of a positive or a negative attitude. That is our only possession. Things happen, facts factualize, and deeds are done, these being all givens. It is only the quality of our attitude that makes us who we are. A consistently positive attitude is our choice of happiness and a similarly consistent negative attitude is our choice of our unhappiness. That is all that we are, that single and significant choice. The fortunes of fate cannot touch that inner resolve, it is ours to keep, if we so choose. The crunch occurs though when one recognizes that with that resolve comes responsibility, and very few want that. Most people perpetually fluctuate in-between, sometimes choosing the positive and sometimes the negative. It is as a great future statesman may yet say, 'people are only about as happy as they allow themselves to be,' and that naturally comes with an appropriate addendum, namely that 'some are never perfectly happy unless they are thoroughly miserable.' The happy few are always happy and preternaturally cheerful, that being their choice, and the miserable majority are always unhappy, that being their choice. This is the greatest democracy of all, the equal possession of choice to all."

"Absolutely perfect, Socrates," Nicias affirms, "happiness is always there for the having, an amazing choice indeed. What you say Socrates is spellbinding but, getting back to reality, the debate tomorrow will surely go against restraint and our precious forces will be sacrificed on distant Sicily. I will do my best." With that Nicias stands, taking the hand of the boy and they begin to walk away. The boy looks back to Socrates who smiles and winks saying, "Young man, I know that you will always do your best."

☆ ☆ ☆ ☆ ☆

Athens is in an uproar. The war has dragged on for far too long and the costs of dead and material are becoming unbearable. A bold move is thought to be required in order to force a resolution. The defensive passivity of Pericles' strategy has garnered no passive results. The concentration of rural folks within the walls of the city has led to a plague that takes 30% of the population, depleting all sectors of society, be it hoplites, rowers, craftsmen, domestics, women, children, and political leaders. A more active war strategy needs to be pushed forward. The Spartans needed to be outwitted, outfought, and brought to heel so that Athens could resume its position of power at the center of the Delian League. The accelerating pace of dwindling reserves needed to be reversed and prosperity returned to the greatest city in the world. Such was the consensus but issues remained in terms of the tactical details of implementation. How could the war be won? This protracted conflict was to no one's liking, save perhaps the arms makers. A war council has been convened before the Assembly and two distinctly separate points of view are offered.

One view was presented by Nicias, a general of solid credentials and proven reputation, and the other by Alcibiades, a newly elected commander with no credentials and questionable reputation. He was hot for an attack against wealthy Sicily. This island though was comprised of competing cities. Syracuse was a Spartan colony but numerous smaller towns resented their imposition and were ripe for revolt. A new alignment with Athens would surely be their foremost desire. The opportunity was at hand to foment trouble in Sparta's rear and then achieve tactical advantage to its front. The projection against Sicily was dreamt up as a lever against the underlying asymmetry of the combatants. One being naval, the other hoplite, it would be necessary to force proxy fights. Reduce Spartan allies and the way would be cleared for their inevitable defeat. The level of wishful thinking could not be properly appreciated at the time but it is fair to say that the Sicilian Expedition in its full splendor turned out to be a perfectly orchestrated and immaculate debacle.

The first speaker in front of the Assembly is Nicias. "Citizens, we are gathered here today to decide upon major issues confronting our beloved city of Athens. We are in the midst of a great war with our enemies and we have every expectation in our final victory. Many are allied against us and we must be careful to think and act in a way that more fully ensures that victory. The issue is how we should prosecute this war with Sparta. It has been vigorously suggested that we marshal a large fleet and proceed to Sicily and subdue the allies of our enemy. The rich city of Syracuse is ours for the taking, so it is claimed, and the many Sicilian enemies of Syracuse will assist us in our rightful struggle against tyranny. Large sums of money have already been promised. Much will be done, presumably. Sparta will be divested of a major ally, Sicily will become part of the Athenian Empire, and we will make a lot of money, so goes the argument. All well and good, perhaps, a seemingly very good idea and an assuredly equally bad reality. I counsel against such folly. …keep what you have and not risk it for advantages which are dubious in themselves… (6.9) We have enemies aplenty nearby without venturing so far to pick a fight with a new one. Do we know for sure that Syracuse's hold on Sicily can be broken and that Athenians would be welcomed across the island? That little village that promised us so much money, is that to be believed? I doubt it. It's always as easy to promise as it is difficult to deliver. I have serious doubts. Sicily is just too far away, our battle is with Sparta. Let us concentrate there. We have only recently been relieved of the horror of the plague and, while we are very much recovered, are we as strong as we think we are to risk such a far flung adventure? I counsel caution. Men of age and reason, talk to your sons who are so hot for this unnecessary fight. It is so much easier to defend one's own homeland than to attack someone else's. The dangers are just too great to expect such an easy victory, as these young hotheads would presume. Let us quit with the nonsense of foreign conquest and mind our own business. The balance of power in our Empire depends upon it. Vote No to this rush into distant uncertainty and possible calamity."

Nicias bows and sits down among scattered cheers and significant shouts and jeers among the youth. They are shouts of "coward, old man, and loser." Alcibiades leaps up and rushes to the forefront. He is dressed in the rather inappropriate attire of full military armor. A great roar goes up as the hotheads acknowledge their handsome hero. The ladies swoon as he struts about and his magnetic good looks keep them mesmerized. As the crowd noise subsides Alcibiades begins to speak, his lisp a little unnerving.

He immediately taunts his rival. "Nicias, you poor, pathetic, loser. Might I suggest, a girly-man." A roar goes up from the assembly. "Are you that weak and feeble minded to think that we great Athenians, the greatest people on earth, can't easily do exactly what we want, especially to a backwater like Syracuse, and extend our Empire to Sicily, Carthage, and Rome? I myself, as witnessed at the Olympic Games with my seven chariot entries, am brave enough to single-handedly lead us to victory against the Syracusans. …if we cease to rule others, we shall be in danger of being ruled ourselves… (6.18) Just daring and courage and a few good men and the deed is done. We're home in no time, having been welcomed and embraced as liberators. Sparta's alliance will be reduced and we are all the richer. I am the man to do all of this for the Athenian people." Another roar of approval erupts. Nicias turns away in disgust and resignation. "Furthermore, our strategic interests are at stake. Sicily controls 60% of the world's known reserves of olive oil. Our economy depends on that oil. We need to secure the olive oil fields of Sicily in order to ensure the prosperity of the Athenian way of life. And need I remind you, the Syracusans once hired an assassin to kill my daddy. Let us not forget this outrage. We must now seek revenge! Also, as the world's first and only democracy, we must fight to impose democracy upon others and then these Sicilians will be better able to do exactly what we tell them. Let the men of Nicias' generation get out of the way and sit and do nothing as we young men rise to the challenge of making war upon Sicily. Let us Vote Yes for War!" A final roar of approval ensues and the decision is made. War against the distant islanders it will be. …everyone fell in love with the enterprise… (6.24)

☆ ☆ ☆ ☆ ☆

After the heated events of the day, a raucous drinking party is in the final stages of disarray. Everyone is clustered around the ever dynamic and good-looking hero of the day, Alcibiades. All are nearly entirely in the bag, drunken to the gills, with nary a single coherent thought possible among them, save the impotent notions of fornication with the scantily clad flute girls. Piles of lumpen humanity are littered on the floor offering little threat of carnal congress. Lost between eager desire and futile consummation the fallen studs limp nowhere. Dyclyssides, the gelding with attitude, as told by the learned Sophist Parmenides, is talking to the resplendent and stupored Alcibiades. "That speech today was the best Alcibiades. We can now go to war and bring great glory to Athens and have fun and make some money too. The gods are good. It's going to be the best. By the way, what was that about strategic olive oil reserves? I thought we had all the olive oil that we can possibly use. Also, did the Syracusans ever actually try to kill your father? I never heard that one."

Alcibiades slurs his lisp. "Dyclyss, you big idiot, are you so naïve as all that? In a democracy you gotta make things up so that the gullible and corruptible people, like yourself, will believe on faith alone. Lies are best told in a democracy and big lies work the very best. The bigger the lie, the harder it is not to believe. It's pure phantasy, a work of the imagination, Socrates would be proud, but it's only human nature. The securing of the olive oil fields is just an excuse. The war will be over and done with before anyone knows that Sicily has no fields at all, but they're big on anchovies. That thing about the Syracusans attempting to assassinate my daddy is just phooey. I made that up too on the spot, it sounded good and that got the biggest applause. So, quit with the details, rumors are always best that are made up to fit the democratic occasion, and now we have a good excuse, I mean justification, all made up, for going to war, for killing lots of people for no good reason at all. Now it's all the responsibility of the people, they voted, the greatest democracy in the world after all, and we can do anything we want. It's called a blank check and getting away scot-free."

Deciding that fresh air will do him some good, Alcibiades stumbles to his feet and exits to the outdoors, staggering into the street. Socrates, ironically, or coincidentally, is ambling by. Alcibiades is startled and thinks to turn and run but remains.

Alcibiades has a vowel movement. "Wall, Socraat, that wasr quite a speeech I gaave todaay, warn't it? Eveeryboody looved it, they all toold mee soo."

Socrates calmly and soberly responds. "Son, you are a very gifted child, but this war of yours, this war of liberation and profit, as you think it to be, can only end in disaster. You are carrying the banner of evil and all those who flock to you, hoping to be like you, will suffer the most. Better could have been expected of you but you have chosen poorly, choosing the vainglory tinsel of popularity and personal deceit. I weep for the innocent. One day perhaps the slaughtered Melians will sing from their mass grave the praises of death as our city may deserve their retribution. Go, do what you must. My concerns can no longer have anything to do with you but only with those who will suffer so much, the innocent." Socrates walks away. Alcibiades puts his hands to his head and appears to weep.

As the son of Thucydides, I weep too with the thought of this freely elected march into doom. But so it was, the Athenians decided enthusiastically upon expanded war and the invasion of Sicily was set, as everyone fell in love with the enterprise. A great fleet was amassed and times were good as the killing had yet to begin. But, as democratic fickle is want to do, the Athenians decided to hedge their bets and to go in two directions at once. It was judged prudent that there would be a two-headed command. The outspoken rivals, Nicias and Alcibiades, were to be co-leaders, to balance the excesses of the one against the other, I suppose. Lampsacus was added as a third general, thinking perhaps that he could mediate the inevitable fight that would arise between the other two. A three headed Athenian command is just what the Spartan gods would have ordered.

Naval preparations proceed briskly in the harbor of Piraeus as everyone cheerfully works at the task at hand being so happy that the excursion to Sicily is about to begin. But things immediately go poorly, in fact, very poorly. In the midst of final preparation, the city awoke one morning to a great horror. Being a deeply religious people, intent upon placating the gods for their own salvation, observant of omens and auspices, the citizens were presented with the spectacle of the mutilation of the Hermes, the little statues of holy reverence that each household placed at the front of the home for protection from wandering evil spirits. The vandals had smashed these religious icons in the night and presented an incredibly bad omen for the pending military expedition to Sicily. Even though Alcibiades was at the height of his popularity, he had collected along the way many personal enemies, and it was ever so natural to assume that he must have had something to do with this unprecedented religious outrage. Who else had such audacity? Everything is in turmoil. The fleet is set to sail, Alcibiades is to be a general, but this crime against religion has not been settled. The people decide poorly again. Alcibiades is charged with the crime of sacrilege but sails with the fleet anyway. But ominous second thoughts prevail and the prison ship *Salaminia* sails to intercept Alcibiades as he has been charged with a capital crime that requires execution. The most handsome man in Athens may lose his head. As so many had come to expect, the war goes badly and is quickly on the road to complete annihilation. Never had so many perished so ignobly in pursuit of such a poorly conceived distant war of opportunism. The defeat was as complete as expectation fell short of reality. The fleet was destroyed only to be reinforced by a second fleet that was equally destroyed. Plan A was supported by a surge to a second Plan A. But Alcibiades survived. A bounty was put on his head but he escapes capture from the *Salaminia*.

☆ ☆ ☆ ☆ ☆

A detailed account of the Sicilian Expedition would reveal a perfect storm of failure as the euphoria of early expectation fell victim to the horror of complete defeat. Alcibiades and Nicias quarreled as was to be expected and the initial assumption of support from much of Sicily that was hostile to Syracuse proved to be entirely without merit. When the locals saw the size of the Athenian force their quick thinking led them to believe that a local overlord was far superior to a distant tyranny. Essential aid and sustenance were denied to the Athenians by the very presumptive beneficiaries of this distant military action. Initial failure was occasioned by the arrival of the *Salaminia* with orders to remove Alcibiades to Athens to face criminal charges. He slithered free of any awaiting shackles and made his way to the Peloponnesus. Nicias is left in command with Lamachus who then gets himself killed. Nicias now alone commands a military expedition that with each passing day is more and more doomed to total failure. He attempts to lay siege to Syracuse by land and sea but a tactical incompetence coupled with a liver disease renders him incapable of victory. He hoped to be recalled by Athens and the mission ended but more of the same was in order. Another fleet, a surge, as it were, was sent to rescue the first as the democratic vote found defeat to be inconceivable. The Syracusans would be defeated by the great Athenian Empire, so the people willed. Wishing can easily be but an empty thought without a prayer.

As a military commander, charged with the safety and success of his forces, Nicias found himself in a personal bind. As the possibility of military success receded he thought that he would be held responsible before the Athenian Assembly and the verdict of death loomed largely. At the point where it was still possible to retreat and save some of the army and navy, he decided instead to fight to the end. A lunar eclipse intervened and convinced the reluctant Nicias to an even greater reluctance and delay. Syracusans sensed the weakness and forced another naval encounter that was conducted with a hoplite assault by Gylippus by land and the Athenian force was destroyed. Picnicking spectators had assembled to witness the final naval carnage. One last spasm of bloodshed ensued. The remaining Athenians, perhaps 30,000 in all, hoped to escape cross country away from Syracuse. Nicias and Demosthenes, a second general, were put to death by vote of the Syracusan Assembly. The remaining few thousands of survivors lived only to die in stone quarries where there could be no hope of living for long.

The Sicilian Expedition was the singularly most catastrophic loss that led to the final defeat of the Athenians still years later. Great battles in the middle of wars turn the momentum from one side to the other and, while much fight is left in the eventual loser, defeat is perfectly ordained. Thucydides, the Historian, my father, said it well. "This was the greatest Hellenic achievement of any in this war, or, in my opinion, in Hellenic history: at once glorious to the victors, and most calamitous to the conquered. They were beaten at all points and altogether; all that they suffered was great; they were destroyed, as the saying is, with a total destruction, their fleet, their army—everything was destroyed, and few out of many returned home. Such were the events in Sicily." (7.87)

☆ ☆ ☆ ☆ ☆

Alcibiades' command in Sicily achieved the height of perfect failure. The intelligence reports proved to be in fundamental error, more wishful thinking than anything resembling hard fact. Sicilian discontent was dramatically less than anticipated, as Syracusan overlords were clearly preferable after all to Athenian adventurers. The town with all the money proved to chimerically destitute of all but well tailored lies of deception. Finally, the fighting Athenians themselves proved to be effectively inept. They had been misled simply because they had chosen to be party to the deception. It just felt right so it must be so but with the unhappy intrusion of reality these feelings were crushed under the weight of deadly facts. A militarily powerful nation often believes itself to be invincible and it is then that it is subject to a lesser power that it had thought to be worthy only of contempt. Of course with any presumption of invincibility there goes a heavy dose of stupidity and with that there is little to be done until the whole disaster runs its course and the harvests of war collected. Such was the Athenian experience in Sicily and upon this failure would rest the responsibility for final defeat.

Alcibiades' full implication prompted him to deep thought and it did not take an animated imagination to realize that it was time to save his own skin. He fled from Athenian justice. With loyalty to himself alone, he slipped away in the night and headed to the Peloponnese, home of the Spartans. Some tricky maneuvering would be in order. He makes his way to the Athenian arch-enemy and thus begins a life on the run that would end only with his death. Using some quick thinking and fertile imagination he expected to ingratiate himself. As an ex-Athenian commander he could be immensely helpful to the Spartan cause. The first obstacle would be getting a hearing but being so good-looking, even though a bit tattered, may work the same wonders that had always cleared the way. He came across a Spartan guard, who barks, "Stop! Who goes there? Helot scum?" The guard takes a closer look. "You look rather strange. Good looking people are not to be seen here. You don't look like the filthy Helots so who are you and state your business."

"I am Alcibiades the forsaken Athenian, friend of Sparta."

The guard is astonished. "Holy schnikes, what are you doing here? We're at war, you Athenian bastard."

"I've come to advise the Spartans on the proper way to defeat the Athenians."

The guard chuckles. "Oh, ya? That's a good one."

Alcibiades extends his arms in submission. "Here, arrest me, but please take me to the King."

The guard is perplexed. "Well, hold on, I'll have to consult with my superior." He turns and shouts to another guard who is sleeping leaned up against a tree. "Hey, Butch, this is Alcibiades from Athens, he wants to see the King. What should I do?"

The second guard yawns. "You could kill him but, ah heck, just send him up the road, let someone else handle the renegade."

The first guard points up the road. "On your way." Alcibiades hurries along.

The kingship of Sparta was unique as it had not one but two kings, as remarked earlier. It was a practical arrangement based upon the requirements of military preparedness. Ever vigilant in its suppression of resident slaves, the Helots, the basis of the city's economic viability, the Spartan army was continually in training. This was a professional hoplite army that was in fact invincible, without pretense or presumption. It trained to the highest level of readiness yet the stated Spartan policy was to be very reluctant to deploy. Be ready but not necessarily willing was a defensive policy that ensured that no strength would be sacrificed without ultimate justification. Defense and not offense, maintaining the home front and not foreign conquest, minding their own business, was the Spartan key to survival and prosperity. With the army in perpetual training, one king commanded in the field, and the other stayed home to attend to internal political affairs, and then annually the roles were reversed. This offsetting power sharing ensured strong leadership at the head of the army and equally strong leadership at home, with neither king being enticed by the allure of absolute power, that entangling elixir of glory, that would prove to be the end of so many kingdoms in the years and centuries to come. The kings served the greater good and not the self-interest of personal gain. Being two rather than one, they were also immediately accountable, that condition of life that marshals decency and respect rather than the indecency and lack of respect of the single king become tyrant.

Alcibiades had made his way safely to the city center of Sparta as after all he posed no threat, being but one without means or wherewithal. He is brought before King Agis, who presides over a gathering of Spartan elders, and carries on the interrogation personally. There is something of the element of the farce attendant upon this interview as the notion of the renowned Athenian Alcibiades coming hat in hand before the Spartan War Council is truly farfetched, if not absurd, but here he stands ready to answer for himself.

The King begins. "What brings you this way, young Alcibiades? Our reports have it that you were the leading advocate for the Athenian troublemaking cruise to Sicily. Things go badly for you?"

Alcibiades responds firmly. "Yes, you are right. I did support that action, but the fickle democratic mob in Athens turned on me. This shows the superiority of oligarchy, or two-headed monarchy, as you have it here in Sparta. ...democracy...is a patent absurdity... (6.89) Let the good people rule and not the low life swine that know nothing. For the treachery against me, the Athenians will pay. I have come here to offer you advice as to the best way to defeat those Attic cutthroats."

King Agis somewhat amused. "Well, that's interesting. Why should we believe you? Maybe you're just a spy up to no good. Your reputation precedes you here and it's bad. It is said that for such a good looking man you are the worst of troublemakers. Your debaucheries are legendary, one could even say, epic. Only the gods could fornicate like you. You come to us poorly recommended. As an Athenian we ought to execute you on the spot with no questions asked. That's apparently what your colleagues in Athens would prefer. That bounty on your head would be worth more than your probably flawed advice could ever be. But, enough of this, go ahead, explain yourself. Why should we trust you?"

Alcibiades says emphatically. "Don't trust me at all, just evaluate objectively the merits of the strategy that I'm going to propose. Think for yourselves, use a little imagination, and you will see the tactical advantage. If it makes sense, OK, if not I will be on my way."

King Agis has a more serious expression. "Go on."

"First off, the Athenians will get bogged down in Sicily. The battle there is nothing like they foolishly expected. They thought it would be easy, that they would be received as liberators by most Sicilians, and that they would make some easy money. All of that is proving to be not so easy. Also, Nicias is a reluctant fool and will lead them nowhere. He's slow to move and oblivious of the obvious. My advice to you is to send an experienced Spartan general to take charge of the forces of your Sicilian allies. Send someone who will act quickly and decisively and the battle will be won. Athenian losses will be catastrophic. They will think that they are winning right up to the very moment of their total defeat."

King Agis ponders. "Interesting, go on."

Alcibiades is confident in his winning ways. "Secondly, bear with me on this one, but you Spartans are very predictable. You make your annual pilgrimage to Attica to destroy crops, forcing the Athenians to hide behind their walls, and then you come home. Damage, surely, victory, never. Fortify Decelea with a permanent garrison of Spartan hoplites. Keep the pressure on the Athenians year round just 10 miles from the city. Also, you have your Helots, we, I mean, Athenians, have their own captive slaves with a similar hostility. They have a bunch of Melian slaves that seem to be always up to no good. If you fortified Decelea that would serve as a haven for run-away slaves, encouraging more to do the same. This would be a permanent thorn in Athenian activities and create a political division between landowners and city dwellers. It would serve as an internal cancer with deadly consequences. That is my advice."

Those gathered have expressions of perplexed thought, the look of thinking for oneself. The clarity, precision, and brevity of this tactical proposal is startling and of course it makes perfect sense. The King responds. "Very, very interesting. We will consider it." The King in a flash already recognizes the validity of the proposal and knows it will be approved under his leadership. His attitude becomes friendly. "Sparta will offer you a place to live. Mind your own business, stay out of trouble, and perhaps do yourself some good and become a Spartan, after all that strange name of yours, Alcibiades, is Spartan in origin. May I call you Al?"

"Certainly, Al it will be. I look forward to becoming a Spartan in more than name alone."

☆ ☆ ☆ ☆ ☆

Alcibiades did in fact live the Spartan life, taking perfectly to the cold waters of perpetual military training. The days were as full as the nights were short, with predawn rise, cold bath, athletic exercise, black broth for lunch which entailed the entrails of anything that had ever lived, then more athletic exercise, weapons polishing, more black broth with a little head cheese for texture, and then early to bed and early to rise as day followed day in the interminable repetition and reiteration of the same. Long hair was the standard so as to present an even more ferocious visage in battle and with all of this Alcibiades the Athenian was transmogrified into Alcibiades the Spartan. All alike marveled at the transformation of the pretty boy into the pretty awful looking warrior beast. People thought of him as the perfect chameleon and, as was quickly rumored throughout the land, the man with the enormous member.

Our transformed hero made a good showing in Sparta. He lived the life and his advice to King Agis was tactically perfect. Gylippus was sent to take charge of Sicilian defenses and the Athenian defeat was total. Decelea was fortified and severe damage inflicted upon the Athenians throughout the year. But Al would be Al and he may have looked Spartan but he was purely Alcibiades. King Agis' generosity would not be reciprocated. He led the Spartan army in the field and left behind his beautiful queen, Timea. The King's absence left opportunity for the lecherous Alcibiades to do his deed or, more precisely, plant his seed where it surely didn't belong.

Timea, the queen of King Agis, was enamored of the second hand Spartan swashbuckler from the start. She fell hard and thought only of some possible clandestine congress with the Athenian stud. The problem of being the queen could be overcome, so she thought as, after all, love conquers all. His close proximity during his months of field Spartanization drove her nuts. Close yet so far away, there had to be found a way. She had to have him. Little individual privacy was afforded in Spartan society. All and everything was subject to general scrutiny for the common good as nothing escaped the eyes of the ever vigilant watchers. The queen paced pensively, daily, thinking, thinking of a way to have her man. The rarest of opportunities presented itself. Out walking in the middle of the day, a short distance from the city, she took refuge in the shade of a grove of hickory nut trees. Startlingly, the Athenian in question ambled by, alone.

"Hi Al."

Alcibiades responds. "Don't call me Al."

Timea ignores his rebuke. "You are so handsome, Alcibiades, any girl's dream. Please sit by you? Do you love me?"

"Gee whiz, I don't know. I didn't even know that you liked me, but I guess so. Being the Queen I thought you loved the King.

She retorts. "Hell no. Sure he gives me little dangly things but he's too much of a man to love. He's gone most of the time anyway and it's easy for a woman to need more than that. I'm in love with love or at least with screwing. You must come to me tonight. You are just too handsome. I must have you. I will be yours.

Alcibiades shows concern. "Where should I meet you?"

Timea is breathless. "In the King's quarters. The King is gone. Nothing can go wrong. We can be lovers without him knowing. It will be fabulous. I will be yours."

Alcibiades is not convinced. "Oh. What if he finds out?"

Timea says confidently. "Nonsense. He won't care. I am the Queen and you are the most handsome man in Greece. What could go wrong? Nothing. My loins deeply yearn for your presence. Bye, bye, until then. My blood is up already."

"Where in the King's quarters should I come?"

Timea flushed. "Second door on the right past the fountain."

Alcibiades unenthusiastically. "Ok. Bye, bye." Timea flits away. The harmless tryst is set, there can be no untoward consequences as love conquers all. Alcibiades muses to himself. "This handsome thing may be my undoing. How can I ever say No when everyone has already said Yes? The fornication is good but it all may end rather badly. When this thing goes bad I will need to be ready to run. Caught between the lust of the Queen and the power of the King leaves little room to maneuver. But who can say no to the bitch Queen? After all, I am Alcibiades, the most handsome man in Greece."

With nightfall Alcibiades slinks past the fountain and enters the second door on the right which is ajar. Timea is slightly hidden behind drapes across the way. As Alcibiades enters she steps forward. She has on a dog collar with a leash that she tosses to Alcibiades. The rest of her is bound in leather straps. Her large breasts bulge forward, tautly held in place, ready to burst.

Timea wastes no time. "Treat me like a dog, you handsome Alcibiades. Plant your seed deep and bold. I am your royal slut forever! Do me hard!" He goes about his business. She squeals in delight, oblivious to the attention that that may bring. Alcibiades stands behind her, thrusting.

Timea is in a crescendo of staccato ecstasy. "Talk to me dirty, call me names."

Alcibiades huffing and puffing grunts. "Sweet pea, take that you slut-bitch-whore-queen."

But with all things carnal, the anticipation far outstrips the consummating reward as satisfaction immediately gives way to renewed anticipation, as the cycle of desire turns. She wanted it to last ever so much longer but he needed to be on his way, in a hurry, gone in a moment, before any peepers realized that the chameleon with huge member had just sired the son of the king. Good work, to be sure, if you can get it, but fraught with questions of personal longevity. He needed to get his ass out of there before the king had his head. Time to run.

The handsome Alcibiades had worn out his welcome. The King, upon his return from the field, was pleased with neither the timing nor the looks of the baby prince. He disowned it, sure it was not his, as rumors had been easily confirmed. Alcibiades the Spartan was about to become Alcibiades the Persian. He fled east. He made his way to Ionia, the western extreme of the Asian land mass and home to numerous Greek cities, with allegiances to Athens, Sparta, and Persia. He was expectant that his advice to the Great King's representative, Tissaphernes, would be welcome. He knew perfectly well how to defeat both the Spartans and the Athenians. The Persian King could then get back into his coffers the hard cash that now went further west to the Greeks.

☆ ☆ ☆ ☆ ☆

Alcibiades' precipitous flight from Sparta landed him on the road to Persia. While Sparta and Athens taunted each other with the hopes of some sort of military breakthrough, when such was entirely too optimistic in this battle to a draw, a third power lingered on the fringe with a specific agenda of its own. The allied defeat of the Persian King Xerxes many years before was yet remembered as if yesterday and remained unatoned. The puny individualists of the West had defeated a supremely superior tyranny of the East as Persia continued to seethe in humiliation. It looked towards a possible opportunity that would allow the power of the East to absorb the petty states of the West so that a resplendent Persia could sit at the center of the world. Amazingly, and without precedence, Alcibiades found himself in a position to personally influence this geo-political endgame. His chameleon abilities facilitated his showing up near the city of Sardis, the Persian base of operations in Ionia, which was commanded by the overlord Tissaphernes. Of course, Alcibiades' safety could not be guaranteed here and a lot of luck and a little charm would be necessary for him to plead his case before the great satrap. It could never be easy but as long as it was possible all effort would be worth the while. His approach to the city wall is met by an extravagantly bedecked Persian guard, a member of the Immortals, whose appearance far outshines any possible call to immediate arms. He looks good and hopes that all appearances will go untested.

The guard jerks to attention and barks. "Stop! Who goes there? Athenian or Spartan scum?" The guard takes a closer look. "You look rather strange. Good looking people are not to be seen here, except at the King's court. Who are you?"

Alcibiades responds naturally. "I am Alcibiades, friend of Persia, forsaken by both Athens and Sparta." The guard is surprised.

"Holy Ahura-Mazda, that's a mouthful. What are you doing here?"

"I've come to advise the Persians on the right way to defeat the Spartans and the Athenians."

The guard chuckles. "Oh, ya? That's a good one."

Alcibiades submissively extends arms. "Arrest me, but please take me to Tissaphernes."

The guard is dismayed and perplexed. "Well, hold on, I'll have to consult with my superior." He turns and shouts to another guard who is sleeping leaned up against a tree. "Hey, Farhang, this is Alcibiades the Athenian Spartan. He wants to see the big man. What should I do?"

Farhang, the second guard says without interest. "You could kill him but, ah heck, just send him up the road."

The first guard is relieved. "On your way." He points up the road and Alcibiades soon enters through the walls of Sardis.

The plush court of Tissaphernes is ornated with the excessive accoutrements of tyrannical wealth. When all prosperity is absorbed by the center the predictable display is beyond human comprehension as all those of the laboring fringe are sunk into an abysmal squalor that beckons forth a call to some sort of justice, some rectification, but there will be none. The precise center takes all as the rest work into the night of total oblivion. Such was the state of Persia, a misery of the many to serve the pleasure of One. The King and his select lieutenants consolidate a court and an army for self protection as a political and economic system is constituted that brooks no dissent. Into this walked our friend Alcibiades, with hat in hand.

Alcibiades is escorted into the inner sanctum by two fully bedazzling palace guards, dressed to kill, and is brought before the satrap Tissaphernes. Thirty feet from life or death he is stopped and a guard indicates his requirement to kneel before the seated representative of absolute Persian power. Tissaphernes begins the interview. "Well, well, well, the Athenian Alcibiades has honored us with his good looking presence. You do get around. Reports on you are always amusing to read. Are you here as an Athenian or a Spartan, pray tell?"

Alcibiades says obsequiously. "Thank you for the honor of your presence. I come here to help you. I'm neither Athenian nor Spartan, but Persian."

Tissaphernes smirks. "Amusing. How is that?"

"The Athenian democracy has forsaken me and the Spartan oligarchy maligned me. I come here to the Persian tyranny only as Alcibiades, myself."

Tissaphernes is amused. "Interesting. That is well said for such a good looking man but how am I to trust you?"

Alcibiades remains assertive. "Easily. Trust me on my merit."

The satrap replies. "Which is?"

Alcibiades, a little heated, blurts. "I know how to win. The Athenians lost in Sicily not because of me but because they undercut my leadership with that scoundrel Nicias who had no fight left in him. It was because the Athenians didn't trust me enough that that battle was lost. No fault of my own. I then told the Spartans exactly how to win. Send Spartan leadership to Sicily and fortify Decelea. Each action was done with astounding success. But they too didn't trust me enough, so I left."

Tissaphernes comments. "I heard that the king trusted you enough with the queen for you to get her with child, and that you didn't just leave but fled with a second death warrant on your pretty head."

Alcibiades blushing. "She wanted me and I gave it to her, that is all I can say, no fault of my own. Women are women, can't get enough of it, ever. At least the new king won't look like that old sot Agis. My offspring are always rather good-looking, at least that's what I've been told."

Tissaphernes grins openly. "Nice, very nice. What are your intentions here, if I should grant you any intentions at all? Can we expect the new Persian prince to look like you too, or what?"

Alcibiades says boldly. "My intentions are pure."

"We shall see. What is it that is on your mind? Conquest of women or conquest of men?"

Alcibiades, presuming his head is safely to remain place, says. "My goal is purely to promote the interests of the Great King of Persia and you, his representative, here in Sardis. The war that is now raging among Athenians, Spartans, and Persians can easily go in favor of the Persians."

Tissaphernes leans forward. "Well, we've been working on this for years now since those hubristic bastards, I mean Athenians and Spartans in alliance, beat us at Salamis. Xerxes, our king, muttered in his sleep for the rest of his life about those "damn Spartans" and those "damn Athenians.""

Alcibiades more loudly. "Times have changed. There is no alliance, only opportunity for your gain."

Tissaphernes draws back. "If you have anything specific to say, out with it."

"The war is coming down to the success of fleets. The final battle will be naval and ships cost a lot of money which neither side has in abundance. They both look for a unilateral alliance with Persia to bankroll this final push. Play them against each other. Promise to fund each side but do so poorly and irregularly. Promise each of them, let's say, 10 talents a month but pay only 2 talents every third month. Let them waste away against each other as both await salvation from you. The uncertainty will crush each in due course. They can each slaughter the other while in the meantime all moves to your great natural advantage. Simply, sell arms to both sides but never enough to make a difference against you. If you can facilitate your enemies killing each other, it can only be good. It's called the Rumsfeld Doctrine."

Tissaphernes thoughtfully reflects, thinking for himself. "Very, very interesting. I will consider it." The satrap in a flash already recognizes the validity of the proposal and knows that it will be his new policy. His attitude becomes friendly. "Persia will offer you a place to live. Mind your own business, stay out of trouble, and perhaps do yourself some good and become a Persian. May I call you Al?"

Alcibiades is relieved. "Certainly, Al it will be. I look forward to becoming just like a Persian."

☆ ☆ ☆ ☆ ☆

Alcibiades is led away to somewhat extravagant quarters. He inspects his new digs, plopping down on the bed. Immediately there is a slight knock at the door. "Who could that possibly be?" Another knock, he rises and says. "Coming." When he opens the door a girl rushes in with a veil covering her nose and mouth, exceptionally well endowed. She is out of breath and rather frantic.

"Al we must be quick. I must be on my way or I will be missed. Call me Fantabulous. Tonight come to my room, second door on the right past the fountain. I'm off. I love you!" She rushes out the door.

Alcibiades says to himself. "What was that all about? Did she call herself Fantabulous? I guess she was. Odd. Second door on the right past the fountain. Sounds familiar. I wish she wouldn't call me Al. I will have to correct her on that. I bet this has something to do with sex, what else? Poor handsome me."

Alcibiades honors her request for a rendezvous and is seen slinking into the night. He knocks at the second door on the right past the fountain. There is a voice from inside. "Come, come in, quickly." Fantabulous is slightly hidden behind drapes across the way. As Alcibiades enters she steps forward. She has on a dog collar with a leash that she tosses to Alcibiades. The rest of her is bound in leather straps. Her large breasts bulge forward, tautly held in improbable place, ready to burst, so it seemed. Fantabulous pants. "Treat me like a dog, you handsome Alcibiades. Plant your seed deep and bold. I am your slut forever! Do me hard, you beautiful beast!" A raucous fornication scene follows as she squeals in delight, oblivious to the attention that that may bring. Alcibiades goes about his business. She squeals in a paroxysm of desire. "Talk to me dirty, call me names."

"Sweet pea, take that you slut-bitch-whore!" After the frantic coitus has been consummated, they together sit at the side of the bed. Fantabulous, catching her breath, "Al, that was so good. You Greeks can toss a spear like no Persian. Your reputation preceded you and I had to have it. I hope my daddy doesn't find out. He knows everything."

Alcibiades startled, dreading the worst. "Who's your daddy?'

Fantabulous smirking. "I'm his favorite, best out of 69. He calls me punkin. You met him today. He's Tissaphernes. I saw you bow down to him as I bow down to you."

Alcibiades is not amused. "By Zeus, please leave, quickly."

"My daddy says that if I get any prettier he's going to put me in his harem. Ain't that neat? Like awesome, like seriously, like cool? What's a harem?"

"It's a kind of paradise. I'm sure you'll like it, like. But please go for now."

"Gone for now but not forever. We must rut again and again, it is simply fantabodacious. A stud like you is sumptuously superlative. You must spew your seed to spite all the dweesels that come around looking for something that they cannot possibly deserve. I must have you for my own in the name of girls everywhere!"

She flees from the room. Alcibiades sits on the edge of the bed holding his head, massaging his temples. "Does this depravity ever end? Have I ever had enough? It's all an eternal recurrence of the same, over and over. Am I that corrupt? Yes. If I could just be half as good as Pericles, that true father of mine whom I treated so poorly. His love of Aspasia was as pure and without blemish as my quest for any slut along the way is ugly and evil. He loved and cherished as I abuse and discard. And Socrates. Where, oh, where is my most beautiful friend Socrates? He taught me so well to do the right thing always yet I choose instead to always do the wrong thing. Wretched beast that I am, if I had just not been so damn handsome, that is the fault."

☆ ☆ ☆ ☆ ☆

Alcibiades prospered as a Persian, easily adopting the fanciful ways of the Eastern elites, that were rich in dainty food, luxurious fancified retreats, and appreciative females with only one function in life, as they clamored for the attentions of the Athenian renegade stud. Tissaphernes is enamored of the lisping chameleon as Alcibiades' dynamic conversation and tactical insights are superior to his own rather tired and near sighted tactics that gain very little. He can bang his daughter all night long and it is no concern of his. Alcibiades is great company and amusing like no other Persian could possibly be. The varied personal qualities of this product of Pericles and Socrates could hardly be possible in the social tyranny of the Eastern desert. It would be conceivable to think of it in the terms that the quantity of the East was naturally trumped by the quality of the West. Mental strength easily overmatches material brawn. Those singularly strong can have no strength against those superlatively intelligent. Tissaphernes liked Alcibiades indeed.

With all of this in mind, Alcibiades is intent upon his established career of duplicity. No royal favor will go rewarded by the indefatigable upstart. His personal self interest must override any hint of gracious loyalty or respect. He is on the make in whatever senses that could possibly mean. Opportunity always knocks for the charmed lisping handsome man born of privilege and advantage. No astral configuration had ever been so perfectly in order.

☆ ☆ ☆ ☆ ☆

Rumor has it that the Athenian fleet is in the area, needing to brawl. While life has been especially personally good under Persian jurisdiction, it is inconceivable that Alcibiades would remain content if an opportunity for escape and adventure were to arise. He has casually wandered away and finds himself overlooking the fleet of his homeland. He finds himself reluctant. A return home, recourse to his Athenian brethren, would not necessarily be vouchsafed, as he surely must presume that his remaining enemies would be rather numerous. But his popularity was genuine among some, his good looks in tact, and his audacity never to be out done. A meeting is arranged. His return as a tactical commander could win the war and carry forward all hatred that could possibly be heaped his way. Victory is the ticket, to win everything, as to the losers go the heartache, or so he speculated. His chances were good, at least even-steven, and that would be enough to risk all, little knowing that such now was simply impossible.

But the money in the bank for Alcibiades and the Athenians is quite specific. It is believed that the consummate traitor can deliver to the Athenians Persian cash. Kissy-face with Tissaphernes, it is thought that Alcibiades can convince the satrap to throw eastern gold on the side of the Athenians, to fund the fleet sufficiently so as to finally sink the Spartan fleet. With one final battle the Spartans would be undone and the victorious Athenians could return to their democratic wonderland. Such were the hopes riding on the return of Alcibiades. He could deliver the goods or, so it was thought.

Ironically, coincidentally, and amusingly, Dyclyssides, his old nar-do-well buddy, the gelding with attitude that Parmenides had so aptly characterized, was the contact man. He appeared on the path leading up from the beach where the fleet was spending the night. The quarter moon provided just sufficient light so that the two recognized each other and indulged in their customary greeting that was as insincere as it was mutually self-serving. They shake each other's hand and Dyclyssides speaks. "Great to see you Al."

"Don't call me Al."

"OK have it your way, no time to disagree, Alcibiades. We need you back on our side. The Athenian fleet is nearby and I have been sent to you to convince you to return. It's those sulking aristocrats back in Athens that are against you but we in the navy know that you can win and we want you back. We need victories."

Alcibiades breathes deeply and puffs abit. "Interesting. I'm living pretty well here. Surprisingly, Tissaphernes has yet to hear of my personal exploits although it may be just a matter of time but, you know, war is even more fun than sex. You think you want it badly, only to find out ever so quickly that it may be much ado about nothing, as little good comes from either. But, philosophizing aside, being the cause of the deaths of others is still a very great rush indeed."

Dyclyssides chuckles weakly. "That's the charmer, that's the Al, I mean Alcibiades, that we all love. So it's settled, you will return to command the Athenian fleet?"

Alcibiades feigns reluctance. "Yes, I will, if you insist." The night had become darker still as each slinks away, each to his own brooding discontent, to consider the prospects for anything good. The success of our hero is virtually a work of art. He finds a way to land on his feet with his head in place, always. Life indeed was good as the friend of Tissaphernes. But this friendship was tested as Tissaphernes came to doubt Alcibiades' sincerity. Reports were rumored that he was talking to the Athenians and that some sort of double dealing was in the works. These reports were confirmed and an arrest warrant was issued. Our hero had achieved a rare trifecta indeed, as three death warrants from three different authorities had been issued. Athenian, Spartan, and Persian warrants wanted his head, a rare hat trick indeed. But he escapes again. He makes his way back to his Athenian beginning. But, is such a string of luck even possible? Perhaps not.

☆ ☆ ☆ ☆ ☆

A restless night had delivered little resolve to Alcibiades on the verge of a return to his Athenian beginning. Throughout his career of antics, of bullying and berating, of lying and cheating, of blaming others and finding himself faultless, and finally of his complete lack of personal integrity and loyalty to those who cared deeply for him, Alcibiades did have a conscience. The influence of his mentor Socrates had instilled in him the voice of reason, of knowing the right thing, but he had simply ignored this inner call when events dictated otherwise. Fully conscious of his utter depravity, he marched on, and the pending return to Athens equally meant a return to the look of Socrates and an upsurge of guilt and the acknowledgement of his complete failure as a respectable human being. There would be ample cheers and adulation as his former hangers-on would sway public opinion to his favor but the only opinion that mattered was that of his teacher and he already clearly knew that such an opinion could only be one of unmitigated disdain. The Socratic project of self-knowledge had been mangled and mutilated in Alcibiades' will to power. All of this rankled just as much as being a circus act at the court of Tissaphernes. To live his life out as a captive in a degenerate culture of utter sloth and desolate oppression was equally appalling as returning to the judgment of Socrates, but the choice was easy. Return to his countrymen and perhaps win a final victory and all will be forgiven, as any prior sins of depravity would be forgotten.

Alcibiades woke early and slipped out of the city. No one really watched or cared anymore, as his presence had become both routine and without concern. Hurrying along, he came to the place on the path where he had talked during the night and there again stood Dyclyssides, who was the first to speak. "Welcome back, Alcibiades. Let us go meet your people."

"Well enough, but my people once wanted me dead. I'm a little reluctant." They proceeded down to the cliff that overlooked the beached fleet. All were at work with the chores of morning revelry and the task to unbeach the fleet and get on with the final struggle of attrition against the Spartans.

Dyclyssides is reassuring. "We all welcome you. We need a commander. It is time to address the men and let them know of your return." Dyclyssides turns and yells. "Hear one and all!" Some of the men pause from their activities to look. Alcibiades has yet to have been recognized. "Men, today we have a special guest. In our time of trouble, we have often been betrayed by poor leadership. We have suffered from the incompetence and lies of those we trusted. Those days are over. I bring you Alcibiades."

As Alcibiades steps forward there is roar of approval. He extends a hand in a sort of gesture of benediction, signaling for quiet. He resounds for all to hear. "Great warriors of Athens, I have risen and return to you. I am born again." A roar of approval goes up, as the grim spectacle of war fatigue is leavened by a new possibility, a new opportunity and belief that victory is within grasp and all can be done with the savagery of destruction and death. "I come in search of home and victory for my people. Salvation will come through me, I am your savior. Trust me and you shall be saved." Another roar of approval erupts, "The Spartan fleet slinks in the area. It is time to destroy that evil viper. No one beats an Athenian fleet. We fight to final victory, as no one is better at the oar. Spartans are landlubbers who are frightened of the water. We will show them the deep blue. They will break under the Athenian onslaught and will find the cold sea their final resting place. The fishes of the sea will grow fat on Spartan blubber." The renewed roar of approval hits the pitch of frenzy. "Men, we win or we die, now. We must fight like never before, the gods demand nothing less. Fight for freedom, fight for family, fight for city, and row to salvation. Let us risk everything here on a throw of the die as anything less will lead to death for most and enslavement for the rest. Row to Victory! Row, men row!" The climatic roar overwhelms, the hero has returned to offer up deliverance for all. "As commander I propose attack. Man your ships, row boys, and onto glory in Athens." In the maelstrom of ecstasy, the men rush to their ships, renewed to the vision of glory and victory.

Our hero had come full circle. Athenian, Spartan, Persian, and once again Athenian, a Western odyssey of Homeric proportions. But the second time around would be fraught with danger, as the first circle had left many dead and just as many seething. For now though the Commander Alcibiades executed his duties to perfection. The Athenian fleet took to oar with him in command. The Spartan fleet fell for a plausible ploy and before they comprehended their error a perfect defeat was delivered. Alcibiades crushed the Spartan fleet in the most stunning battle of the war. The Battle of Cyzicus will go on to achieve textbook mention as one of the great naval victories of all time. Spartan messengers attempted to deliver home a message from Cyzicus. It was intercepted by the Athenians and read, "Our hopes are at an end. Mindarus is slain. The men starve. We know not what to do." Other victories followed and his star had fully risen, born again. It was time to return home to Athens and to receive the acclaim that was so rightfully his.

☆ ☆ ☆ ☆ ☆

A string of victories at sea lifted the spirits of Athenians who had become accustomed to stinging defeats. The prospects for final victory greatly improved. Alcibiades was the one most responsible. He needed to return home and clear his name and receive the blessing of his countrymen, but circumstances were not perfectly clear. His record of betrayal was exemplary and many thought of that rather than his more recent victories. Alcibiades was concerned for his life. How would he be received? Was he walking into a death trap? Things could easily go very badly, but delay was no longer possible.

The Athenian flotilla slowly made its way into the port of Piraeus. In tow are 200 captured enemy triremes, a tremendous booty by any measure. Boy, could that handsome Alcibiades deliver. What an invigorated surge of emotion to see that after all Athens would win, and Alcibiades would have done it all, traitor be damned. The docks and shore are crowded with jubilant men, women, and children welcoming home their long absent heroes. Much celebration is in order as prospects for the war have improved dramatically, and all to the tactical brilliance of their tarnished favorite son, Alcibiades. His ascendant star could not have shone brighter. His command trireme ties up and he leaps onto the dock dressed in full military regalia. The already boisterous crowd erupts into a shout of welcome and acclaim. Defeat at the hands of the Spartans has been snatched from the jaws of certainty and no one had forgotten the fate of the Melian islanders at the hands of the Athenians. Defeat would mean universal comeuppance as an exact fate ought to be expected for themselves. Relief from the specter of this general annihilation is visibly at hand. How could it have been otherwise? The lisping demi-god Alcibiades is about to speak. But all is not well, as past sins, prior violations, remain in mind. He recognizes in the crowd some very long faces. The hero stands forth, not entirely sure of himself.

"I come home before you today a new man, born again, a man delivered from the tribulations of years of exile. I had nothing to do with the desecration of the Herms. Having been accused and convicted in my absence, I tried to achieve victory in Sicily. The debacle and disaster there was not my fault. Nicias is solely to blame. I did my best and was forsaken."

Someone in the crowd yells. "Please forgive us, Alcibiades, it was our fault, we didn't trust you enough."

Harlote, the whore, adds further sentiment. "Yes, yes, we love you! We are not worthy."

Alcibiades smirks slightly, his ever-present expression, and continues. "This war drags on with misery all around. We need to end it in victory. But first more battles are necessary and I shall deliver." The roar of approval signals the absolute belief in that victory. "My time in the city here must be short. The fleet is in need of my command. We must hurry to meet our destiny. In a week's time we shall sail so make haste in preparation."

Alcibiades' intentions are not pure, or for real. It is true that he may be able to redirect Persian gold in the Athenian direction, but at a very high cost. The democracy must go. The Persian King cannot tolerate a fickle democratic mob when it is so much easier to deal with an oligarchic few of the city's best citizens, meaning richest. The Golden Rule will be imposed. "He who has the gold, rules." A revolution must be brought to bear where the democratic Assembly will be replaced by Thirty Tyrants. The upshot will be that a second civil war will shed blood. Spartan versus Athenian will be augmented by Athenian versus Athenian, domestic killings to the second power. The cheers for the returning prodigal son Alcibiades will be short lived as more terror and violence will surge through the streets, as neighbor attacks neighbor. In the purges that follow as many as 1500 people are murdered, democrats and oligarchs alike. The dawn's revelation of the nightly dead leaves everyone wishing themselves better dead than alive.

☆ ☆ ☆ ☆ ☆

A long night of party making followed with Alcibiades making sundry cameos here and there. He screws one, then another, but there is only so much seed to sow. The old gang of worthless hangers-on are again congregated at the center of which are Dyclyss, Rumy, and Georgi. They swagger into the street and are immediately surrounded by a group of men who hustle them across the way into a darkened room. By single candlelight is seen Hipponicus, ex-father-in-law, payor of huge dowry, and arch enemy of Alcibiades who doesn't recognize him. "Ah ha, my favorite ex-son in law." Alcibiades now recognizes and jolts backward but is moved forward by those behind him. "Defrauder of many, scoundrel to most, traitor to all, and the death of my only daughter. Al, may I call you Al, how goes it? You look a little beaten. The crowd loves you though and that's good for the complexion. We have gathered here tonight to discuss a few loose ends. Please feel free to say nothing, as I will do the talking. A meaningful grunt or a special squeal is all you need to utter. First, I would like to recover the remnants of that large dowry that you received when you destroyed my daughter with grief and embarrassment, but really, you just keep it, I don't care. More importantly, an Open Society for Minding One's Own Business has been formed in your absence, and it may concern you. We call it The Hague, a name that Parmenides recommended, you remember him. It promotes the minding of one's own business both at home and away. It seeks to tell the truth always and to hold accountable those who scheme, deceive, and lie, and then start wars. Terrible, isn't it? Was that a grunt I heard? Oh well. Anyone caught engaged in such activities will be charged as a war criminal and then must stand before the tribunal of The Hague and answer for his behavior. You, my son, will be the first standee, with the three Wit brothers here, Half, Dim, and Nit. But, for now, to show our generosity, you will be allowed to return to the fleet and perhaps save our city its pending doom. So, for now, bye bye, Al. We are watching. Surely, though, you're already a goner, just a matter of time. Have a nice day." The foursome scurry out. Hipponicus rubs his chin in satisfaction.

Alcibiades returned to the fleet in the nick of time. The Spartans had rebuilt and the Persians had unleashed their gold. The combined Spartan/Persian navy was on the hunt for Athenians in general and Alcibiades in particular. Lysander the Spartan and Cyrus the new Persian on the scene had final victory clearly in their sights. But the Athenians were hopeful too, but with less margin for error. In the midst of renewed hope, Alcibiades made a fundamental error. He left command of the fleet in the hands of an underling while he was off raising money with instructions that nothing be done, just stay put and refuse battle. Big mistake. The underling in a fit of either bravado or stupidity did give battle and was defeated. Alcibiades was ultimately to blame and the penalty would be death. There would be no room for judicial maneuvering now. Losing generals were never allowed to peacefully retire. The newly kindled love affair between Alcibiades and Athens had gone to seed. The long simmering mountain of rage against him now erupted. The Hague awaited. It was time to run again.

☆ ☆ ☆ ☆ ☆

Alcibiades ran and Athens fell. The Spartan/Persian alliance achieved final victory at Aegospotami and Athens was brought down. Her fleet was gone, her walls demolished, her empire dismembered, and her survivors in absolute fear of justifiable total retribution. The Melians were much on their minds. Would the Spartan General Lysander do to them what the Athenians had done on the island of Melos? It seemed to be reasonable justice. That was the question. The Spartans deliberated but refused such a final solution. They harkened back to when Athens and Sparta stood together, risking all in the defense of the country against eastern Persian tyranny. The Spartans said No and let the Athenians live. The Athenian carnage on Melos would not be replayed in Athens, still the most beautiful city in the world. Perhaps the Spartans recognized the exemplary genius of the Athenians but now humbled and without the resources of empire for making trouble abroad. More securely tethered the Athenians would continue to have very much to offer. A general death penalty also may have been thought unnecessary simply because the Spartans had acted no better and atrocities abounded on both sides, the natural fruit of civil war. Defeat itself was thought to be sufficient punishment for these surviving Athenians as they could now mull their losses and failed efforts over and over again. The life of humiliation would be their special cross to bear.

☆ ☆ ☆ ☆ ☆

Alcibiades fled to the north, to a villa in Thrace that he had secured with Athenian cash as a safe haven in the event of just such an eventuality that now befell him. He needed to get out of town and get hid quickly. Life though at the villa was without much excitement save the local girls. He was still amazingly good-looking and a throb to any girly-gig in love with love. This time though he ought to have been a little more circumspect. Any girl would do but this time the chieftain's youngest daughter, a local beauty with huge breasts that enormously pleased Alcibiades, was an infinitely poor choice for the rut. With daughters come sons and, in this case, there came a pack of them. Next to the villa stood a small cottage and it was his preferred abode of fornication and accordingly it was here that Al was humping the little princess. A single candle illumined slightly the huffing and puffing and squealing that is so much a delight. But his little ruckus draws attention and the band of brothers surrounded the place with specific intent in their hearts. They know all about the buccaneer Alcibiades and want nothing more than the rescue of their innocent sister and the final demise of the chameleon with huge member.

Tootencommon, the oldest son, barks. "Alcibiades you lecherous bastard. Let that girl go. She wants to have nothing to do with you."

Alcibiades peeks out the window and yells back. "Who are you people? I'm innocent. She wants me bad."

"She is our sister and the daughter of the King of Thrace, our father."

"Oh, I didn't know, my mistake, but she still wants me, she just said so."

"Enough, send her out now."

"No, I shall defend her with my life."

"Well enough, you Athenian swine. Appear and fight like a man."

Alcibiades bellows. "No, I fight like a lion." With that Alcibiades opens the door and is hit in the heart by a javelin and in the genitals by an arrow. He collapses and dies, a fitting end to he who was responsible for the end of so many others.

Thus concluded the life of the great Athenian scoundrel, Alcibiades, the most handsome man in the world, our anti-hero. His virtues were clearly less than his vices but his dynamically confident personality and good looks made him an exceptional character that fit perfectly with the circumstances of the Peloponnesian War. But, looking at the matter, it was those good looks that were his undoing, a rock star before its time, as so many others sought to be near him. His daring exploits of disaster had ample devotees of complicity. When the consequences of failed responsibility were finally meted out, many would hope to scatter.

☆ ☆ ☆ ☆ ☆

The Peloponnesian War ended with the total defeat of the Athenians, something simply inconceivable. The second rate power Sparta had brought down the mighty empire, guerilla fighters had gutted the superpower, and the seemingly weaker had outdone the stronger. The oppressively arrogant had been perfectly humbled. The bully had been gutted and spitted. Someone must be found to blame other than those truly responsible. How had this happened? The final outrage of the war was the judicial proceedings against Socrates. Our persistent gadfly was the one singled out for final responsibility as our collective guilt was to be exonerated. He, of all people, was the one to serve as a scapegoat for the myriad of war boosters who had thought to profit so handsomely and now sought cover.

The day of the trial dawned with the fact that it was going to be hot, very hot. With no breeze and an oppressive sun overhead, the open air courtyard would be a physical trial for everyone. But the charges must be read and judgment passed. Lampoon, the father of the dim-wit Georgiripides, would be the trial judge, a task far beyond his feeble ability but demanded of his wife, the queen of all that involved false rumor and vicious character assassination in our beloved city of Athens. Her boy had fared poorly during the war and she needed to wreck vengeance upon the head of this Socrates, this string puller of the pretty boy Alcibiades whose nickname for her Georgi had done so much to tarnish her fading years. The name had stuck, Asshole of a Chicken. She sought revenge and her weakling husband would be charged with the delivery of the goods. So, Barbarella, matriarch of the family, mother of Georgiripides, the O-ring of a flightless bird, was out to get Socrates, the unholy bastard most responsible for her lifetime of heartburn. Personal vendetta will have achieved a new standard of excellence.

Lampoon was already sweating profusely. The jury and spectators had gathered, nearly everyone in the city, and the trial could begin. He yells, "Quiet, quiet! Let us begin. The day is going to be hot and if we hurry we may beat the worst of the afternoon heat." The crowd quiets and the trial begins. "We are gathered here to hear the charges to be brought by Platypus against Socrates. Please refrain from any loud interruptions. Be kind enough to let us all hear clearly. Platypus you may begin."

Platypus, having the look of a duck with a weird bill, resident bully, leaps to his feet in a frenzied fomentation. "You, you, Socrates, are the cause of all our problems. It is you that caused our defeat at the hands of the Spartans. You are guilty and must die."

Lampoon waves his hand to stop, proclaiming. "Calm down, Platypus. We know you're good at exaggeration, but let's get at the truth as reasonable men. You don't need to get so excited. Make you charges and we will decide. Now, start over and state your case against Socrates without any high feather drama. The truth then will become evident and set us free from the heat."

Platypus calms slightly. "Athens suffered immensely from the war with Sparta and in the end we were defeated. And why? Because we got incredibly poor advice from our generals. Their intelligence reports were all cooked. It was that renegade consort of Socrates', Alcibiades, who talked us into that debacle in Sicily which was the single greatest cause for our final defeat. Let us trace the facts backward. Defeat, Sicily, Alcibiades, and then there sits the bump Socrates. He is the first cause of a chain of events that spelled the end to our great Empire. Alcibiades convinced us that it was in our strategic interest to secure the olive oil fields of Sicily, and he made us believe that that must be so. No one thought to question this claim and as it turned out it was but a fabricated excuse just to convince us when there should have been no convincing. We should have thought for ourselves then but didn't. It was Socrates who taught him how to do this, how to manipulate lies and convert them into something that looked handsome but was really simply pure deception. Socrates taught him how to make the untrue true so that the rest of us would take him at his word because he was so good looking. We were taken in and it is all the fault of Socrates." He points at Socrates.

"You are a corrupter of the youth of Athens and have taught them how to deceive good men like myself. We wanted to believe those lies of Alcibiades and you made us do it. It all sounded so good and profitable."

Lampoon looks at Socrates. "Have you anything to say to this? It all seems right to me. Defend yourself if you can. Great Zeus, it's hot."

Socrates stands, looking towards his accuser. "Platypus you confuse me. Was what you just said an accusation against me or my best defense?"

Platypus is perplexed. "What do you mean? I don't get it."

Socrates replies, letting it go. "Forget it then, it doesn't matter. Let us continue. Can I speak at length without interruption, or will I be allowed to speak only in bits and pieces? Are you still in a hurry? Is there going to be a rush to judgment? Has the verdict already been made? Has the heat of the day already gotten to you?"

Lampoon is not amused. "Quit with all the questions. We want answers not questions. You may speak at length and of course this is a fair trial to find the truth, nothing has been rigged like usual. Say whatever you must, we will listen closely and then deliver a final verdict, as best we can. But get on with it, quickly. My sweat drips profusely."

Socrates takes his time. "With the likes of Platypus here, I can see that my reputation is rather tarnished. I have never fared too well in the competitive marketplace where one is supposed to get ahead. In fact, my wife, Xanthippe, says that the only thing I'm good at is failure and she's always right. I don't argue. I concede defeat early and often. My problem is that I'm rather ignorant for my age but I do keep trying to improve myself, always trying to do better and finally learn something. In fact I tried to learn something from Platypus here once a while back and ironically my ignorance only made him mad. I asked him what beauty itself was and he had several very good answers, I thought. He said that beauty was a good horse. Well and good, everybody loves a good horse, but I said, what is beauty itself that makes the horse beautiful? He didn't know. Then he said that beauty was a good looking youth, like Alcibiades. Well and good, I said but what is it that makes the boy beautiful? He didn't know. Then he said that beauty was a pile of money. Well and good, but what is beauty itself that makes a pile of money beautiful? He didn't know. And then he got mad and started to insult me, warning me to mind my own business, advice that he might have taken himself. Others witnessed this transformation of behavior and I guess that Platypus has carried a grudge ever since. He doesn't care a wit about my so-called corruption of the youth of Athens. He's in it for himself, trying to get even by bringing me before this court, or so he thinks. I must say that all of my questioning of him was a failure as I was no better informed regarding the nature of beauty itself. I was as ignorant as ever, but at least I knew that, and, amazingly, that is no small feat, to know one's own ignorance. This alone has kept me on the path to knowing something, and perhaps even knowing myself a little more. It's a mystery. I continue to look. But, Platypus never got over his rage. I failed again and my wife told me so and she was right again. I don't argue with her. But let's move on to the real reasons for our defeat at the hands of the Spartans. Simply, arrogant overreach."

Lampoon is drenched in sweat. "Socrates, boy you are a talker. It's early but we need to take a short break by way of refreshments and think this through a little. Beauty itself? What on earth could that be? It's puzzling. I thought that beauty itself was the Parthenon but that can only be but one example of beauty itself. So many things are beautiful that I suppose that it can't be any one thing. I'm at a loss. By way of contrast, of course, our defeat is ugly indeed, no beauty there. I need a drink." The jury mills about, breaking up into small groups, as refreshments are served. Platypus leers in the direction of Socrates. People point at his enflamed complexion. He is not happy. Above the buzz Socrates waves to a small group of young men. He is heard to say. "Plato, thanks for coming."

The pandemonium of intermission begins to subside as a distinguished figure rises at the front of the jury. He is whitened with age and slightly stooped as a hush comes over the jurors. It is the celebrated Ictinous, the designer and builder of the Parthenon. Universally acclaimed as a genius of architecture, this life long friend of Socrates seeks to speak on the defendant's behalf.

"Gentlemen of the jury, I wish to speak of my friend Socrates and relate to you what he has meant for me. When Pericles first approached me with the thought of building a Temple to Athena he suggested that I first of all go speak with Socrates. He was rather vague about this as Socrates was neither a designer nor builder but I took his suggestion and spoke with him numerous times over an extended period of time as the plans for the building were being drawn up, before a single stone was set into place. Frankly, the Parthenon, which we now see across the way, atop the Acropolis, I could not have completed without his guidance. You may ask, what was that guidance? He asked me what I intended the building to be. I didn't rightly know, hadn't thought about it much. I made up some stuff and said it should be pretty and like other temples in Greece. He asked me what the pretty was, I didn't know. So we started over and he suggested that the pretty was part of the beautiful and that we should first ask about the beautiful itself. Well, I was clueless as you can easily imagine. He thought it must be some sort of essential proportion, something wherein the many parts perfectly reflect a single whole, something where the parts are perfectly subsumed by the whole as, for example, the nose, mouth, chin, eyes, and hair and not explicitly seen but rather one simply sees a beautiful face. I had myself never considered such a thing and it took me by surprise that one could think so deeply about things, but it did make a lot of sense to me, for the first time. This insight of the essential proportion instructed me in every bit of design and construction as I never lost sight of the comprehension of the whole with respect to the parts. One doesn't build like this by cobbling one part to the next but rather by keeping in mind an overall perfection into which all parts must be placed. There was established a certain rhythm of part to whole that murmured through my mind throughout the entire process, a sort of inner voice that still infuses my thoughts. It's what makes me happy. This insight has been helpful in other respects as well as thinking in terms of an essential proportion between parts and the whole is universally important."

"There is another way of saying this that has broad political and philosophical implications. Thinking in terms of wholes and parts lends itself to thinking in terms of the general and the particular, as they may be the same thing. The special task, a sort of infinite task, is to see the one then the other as then simultaneously seeing both. To regard only the general is to be left in the self-induced mental fog of the mystic and to regard only the particular is to be grounded in a cave-like reality that is without daylight. It is in thinking them together that philosophical understanding becomes possible. This is by nature extended to the reality of political life. It is the seeing the long term and the short term simultaneously, the common interest and the special interest together. An imbalance to either one or the other will leave one fighting ideological battles that are without merit regardless of how fervently either the one side or the other is believed and proclaimed. Ideology is the lazy man's presumption to philosophical truth. There are no short cuts here."

"All of this may have very important consequences. To recognize, to see, the beautiful itself, is to mentally grasp an invariant and essential structure, a sort of essence or concept, which is first recognized as the culmination of an intellectual process. Looking about I see things here and there without a clear understanding as to what they may or many not be but, in a continuing process of comparison, the essential structure emerges as an act of mental life. There is a shift of attention from the thing that materially approximates the concept until I choose to see the concept alone and thereby enter the dimension of conceptual thinking. Shifting from looking at beautiful things,

I intellectually grasp the conceptual essence of the beautiful itself. Having achieved the fundamental breakthrough of the concept, it is then possible to enter a domain that is constituted of concepts alone. A conceptual language ensues that for the first time allows one to think for oneself as one has entered the world of consciousness and then self-consciousness, which is the explicit awareness of this possibility. This all then constitutes who and what we are as human beings. I know none of this on my own but only through the wisdom of Socrates as he spoke about the beautiful. But none of this matters here as my real reason for choosing to speak has little to do with the beautiful but very much more to do with the ugly, the perfectly ugly."

"In my mind, there was no greater unsung hero in Athens during the plague at the beginning of the war than Socrates. It's hard to imagine now exactly how horrible conditions were then when so many died, including Pericles. Before his death he asked me to design and build some pits, some mass graves, to consume the dead as quickly as possible. The first concern was the removal of corpses. I spoke again with Socrates and we agreed that these bodies needed to be disposed of immediately as they contributed to further death. Some of you sitting here today are alive because of these efforts. This man that you think to condemn never tired of the daily task of collection and burial, and he was especially careful with children, making sure that their burial was proper and respectful even in a mass grave. He worked until the daily job was done. While most others shunned this labor for the dead, thinking perhaps to save themselves, Socrates never cared about himself, never quit until the daily toll was properly buried. While our losses were overwhelming, it is my heartfelt belief that many more would have succumbed had it not been for the labor of Socrates. If you vote against him, be fully aware that you simply know not what you do."

"At the conclusion of these long days shrouded in the heartache of death, the two of us would sit awhile and think a little bit together. Guess what was on his mind? The beautiful. To encourage me he was always sure to compliment me on my work on the Parthenon. He said it was beautiful, just simply beautiful. With such high praise I was perfectly happy, but of course it was his insight that had made it what it is."

"Oh, by the way, one last little thing. A short time after the plague had subsided Socrates spoke with a fervor and seriousness that was absolutely mystifying to me. I remember the words but nothing of its final meaning. He said that this essential proportion had further consequences, this grasping of the whole and its parts simultaneously, with each immediately disclosing the reality of the other as a single insight. This proportion extended into the dimension of time. It was the matter of seeing together the now of the living present and the full totality of eternal time itself. It was something like seeing all of the universe and the place of oneself all at once. Of course I couldn't do such a thing but it set me to thinking as thinking itself is a sort of analogue to this seeing. Socrates said that it took a fair amount of practice and concentration but he hoped that it could be done because this was simultaneously a portal through which lay a dimension simply surpassing any comprehension. It was where an essential proportion became a perfect and eternal proportion. He couldn't say much about it but he had given it a name, he called it the Idea of the Good. It is where space and time become one, where one sees that All is One and One is All, where divinity infuses all of being in a single panoramic ray of eternality. I haven't a clue as to what all of this could mean but its all that I think about now. It may be like seeing like a god, I don't know. Maybe with enough practice and focus I will get it too someday. Of course all of this would be the end of war." Turning to Socrates, Ictinous says, "Thank you."

A disturbing quiet had come over the jury until Dyclyssides leaps up. "Shut up you old wind bag. I'm the smartest man in the world and I don't know what you're talking about, it must be perfect nonsense. The man's guilty, anybody can see that because I said so, kiss my ass. He's just a busybody minding the business of others. On with the trial, what does Ictinous know? On to the verdict of death!" He sits down in a huff and puffs himself up as laughter is heard all around. But it is time for Socrates to speak on his own behalf and in using the voice of reason hoping to instruct the jury to a rightful verdict

Socrates begins anew. "At the end of the war, when all those initial expectations of easy and quick victory have been crushed against the hard facts, when ideological overkill and tactical stupidity have prevailed, when Plan A collapses of its own dead weight, there comes the time to find scapegoats. Of course the truly responsible have all left the city with the best of their profits. So it is to the innocent that they need to turn to get themselves off the hook, anybody will do here. My own special quest for knowledge easily has become a special target for your fabrications. Blaming anyone else is infinitely better than recognizing one's own complicity. The truth is that wars are always amazingly good in the beginning and incredibly bad in the end." There is some rumbling to be heard among the people of the jury and many could not be happy with the Socratic line of thinking. "The charges against me claim that I was responsible for the activities of Alcibiades regarding the Sicilian disaster. He was a friend, student, and fellow soldier, but I myself had nothing to do with his and your desires towards Sicily. I am for the most part a private individual, shunning the corrupting influence of political life, but I was never so public in my condemnation than in my warning of the disaster that would await us in Sicily. It was the wrong fight at the wrong place and at the wrong time. It was clear that this invasion was but a cover for a small group of true believers in the righteousness of the Athenian Empire to impose its will upon unsuspecting innocent people elsewhere. The true cost for this arrogance was naturally paid by the dead soldiers who were deceitfully convinced to fight. Our army and navy losses were heartbreaking for the parents who could only grieve and who had been duped by a patriotism that was only a ruse for the profits of a few. How was this possible? Easily. When the money is so big, there is plenty to go around. Talking heads can be bought cheaply and instructed to spin any objection into yet one more reason for war. And, boy could they shout, shouting to drown out any possible reason otherwise. Lies are dressed up as truth so that the happy marching to war may begin. You may have confused good-looking with good-judgment and then let yourselves be led by the nose to go where you did not belong. That is not my fault. My biggest crime is that I made those who thought they knew everything realize that they knew very little indeed. Having done this in public, they easily played the part of buffoon and for that they find me guilty. It's just more of the same, stupidity stacked on arrogance, stacked on overreach, stacked on denied responsibility, stacked on daddy's money. Of course, they are all a bunch of hypocrites. Hyped on a phony patriotism and steeped in beautiful piles of ill-gotten money, they are convinced that the dead of others is just the right price to pay for doing whatever they please. There is only one thing to do here, only one way to step clear of the chintzy lies of war and the preparation for war. We must all think for ourselves."

"A particularly vicious campaign was launched under the heading of 'Support the Troops.' This was an emotionally sanctioned lie that silenced any criticism of the war. Anyone against the war was implied to mean one was somehow therefore against the troops, a patent absurdity, as no one could possibly be against the troops. But the reverse is more the case. In Supporting the Troops one ought to be against a phony distant war. It was a bait and switch that left thousands dead. 'Support the Troops' simply ensured that the propagators of war could go ahead with no real questioning and once we were in deep there would be no turning back. To justify prior dead more dead were sacrificed until war continues only because it continues, as there is no longer any justification but the thought of no longer killing somehow diminishes the sacrifice of those already dead. 'We were waist deep in the Big Muddy and the big fool said to push on.' We are then fighting because we are fighting, a vicious tautology that continues on its own, on and on. Another term for this would be boneheaded stupidity. Since the profiteers will pay no personal price their profits are huge and therein lay the glory of starting wars that others will fight. No harm done if others must die."

There is a loud disturbance and Socrates is forced to sit down. Platypus leaps to his feet, out of breath, "Socrates, who do you think you are? What makes you think that you are so different from the rest of us? Why do you think you are better? This is a democracy, everyone is the same yet you think you're different. Explain yourself to the jury, and quickly, you arrogant nay-sayer."

"Platypus, I'm so sorry that you think that way but I do love my city of Athens, as much as anyone. There is nothing that I would not do on her behalf. In our democracy, everyone wants an opinion but very few can handle responsibility. But when mere opinion is hoping to get something for nothing, to impose a will upon someone else, for one's own gain, then that opinion is mistaken. Truly, I have only sought to mind my own business, to remain within the private domain of my personal life and to look at the world and to think deeply regarding the true and the false. If you say that I am different, it is because I concern myself with only those things that matter with regard to the highest things such as beauty itself, love itself, friendship itself, and finally political rightness itself. There is no money in this, there is no huffing and puffing as a prelude to war, but instead only a minding of oneself and a coming to know thyself just a little bit better. I am not better or worse, the same or different, arrogant or not, I am simply myself. Of course, in a democracy this may not mean much, but so be it."

Platypus is exacerbated. "Socrates will you ever quit with your sniveling? We have heard enough. The day is hot. Let us vote on your guilt and get to the execution."

Lampoon looks to Socrates. "Platypus is right, let's get on with it. If you continue to talk we will all be guilty. We really are only looking for one to serve our purpose. Let us take the vote.

Guilty or not?" Half the jury's arms are raised. A commotion continues for some time, as the counting is finalized. Lampoon announces. "There is one more vote for guilty than for acquittal." He turns to Socrates. "The voice of the people has spoken, this is their desire. You are guilty as charged and the penalty is death, unless you can think of something better."

Socrates smiles. "I would like to thank the people who voted for my acquittal. By such a small margin, a single vote, one more crime is to be committed. Ironically, a one vote democratic majority implicates everyone, as if any one person were to have voted otherwise this permanent offense against philosophy shall have been averted. But the truth is clear here. It is as I have said. The few have corrupted the City and now need cover for their profits. I would like to propose an alternative penalty if that is the wish of the court. My penalty ought to be that I can live the rest of my life doing exactly as I have done, trying to encourage myself and others always to do the right thing. Let me continue to examine my life as that seems to be the most reasonable thing to do and if others were to find some benefit from this let us give a rightful prayer to this gift of divine dispensation."

Lampoon is amazed. "What? Are you nuts? That will never do, we need to have you suffer, the people demand it."

Socrates is resigned. "I suffer for you all and hope that when comeuppance is delivered you remember me in your prayers. Do what you must and in the meantime you can find me alone in prayer for the Melians."

The jury breaks up. Platypus gloats and quacks, Lampoon sweats. Socrates stands and is taken away by guards. Plato and his group throw their hands in the air and lament.

☆ ☆ ☆ ☆ ☆

Due to a misinterpretation of the proper scheduling of a religious observation the execution of Socrates was delayed.

He was taken to a minimum security jail as the arthritis in his knees made the prospect of him running rather remote. A single jailer named Saul was assigned to his supervision and the two got on very well. They became fast friends, thick as thieves, as it were, and later the jailer would say that being in the presence of Socrates gave him an effervescent tingle that charged all his senses and gave him a feeling of perfect well-being, something akin to a religious experience, perhaps something upon which to build a church, if that were conceivable. The Athenian authorities had demanded that there be no coddling of the prisoner, the convicted malcontent, but Saul had no heart for such unnecessary maltreatment and the two instead passed the day in pleasant conversation. Visitors were welcome and most were fledgling students of Socrates who would come armed with yet another plan for escape which would be politely declined. With or without the arthritis there would be no running. Escape would have been rather undignified for such a man of grace and gratitude. To where, to what, to whom? His life had been in the city and his death would follow in due course in the city as well. It had nurtured him and to it he owed everything. When Socrates would refuse yet another plan they would break down in tears and wail away for awhile until emotionally spent and then depart, leaving the two to resume their conversation. One question that concerned Saul was whether the death penalty was a good thing. Did it allow a city to more perfectly rule its citizens? He quickly and embarrassingly realized that it may not be the most comfortable question for a man awaiting the death penalty. He tried to apologize but Socrates would have none of it and replied that it was a perfectly legitimate question. Socrates' answer involved a series of questions. What was the intent of the death penalty? Was it for deterrence, punishment, cruelty, sport, or let-someone-else-pay-for-the-sins of others? This of course made the jailer's head spin and he was lost in confusion. He had thought it to be a simple question. Since most of the time most of us are perfectly lost in confusion it was possible that the intention of the death penalty was all of the above, just pick a suitable justification. It served many needs and since the doomed had no say anyway any excuse would do. But the state sanctioned killing of a human being is a very serious thing as there are consequences. Friends and family often seek revenge and more killings follow which engender even more and the blood that started as but a trickle can easily escalate into a torrent and once a torrent a full civil war will plunge all into a perdition that is a moonless night indeed. Once the killing begins the only thing that is predictable is the unpredictability of the continued killing. Simply, nothing good can come from it but very much that is perfectly bad. There seemed to be no arguing with this so it was left at that. War itself, mass killing, followed the same template.

On the day before the scheduled execution a lone visitor appeared in the late afternoon. Plato would never claim to be Socrates' favorite student, that title belonging to Alcibiades, but of all things he was the most tenacious. He took his teacher very seriously. Philosophy for him was not a late childhood thing to be renounced when the requisites of money making intrude in early adulthood. It was not a verbal game of one-upmanship and public humiliation or a trick for the intellectually gifted, delivered with sarcasm and scorn. No, instead it was a life long odyssey of the spirit to achieve whatever inkling of insight was possible. It was a project of immense proportions to think clearly and distinctly upon all the issues concerning the being human in a world of an infinite historical horizon. So it was perfectly appropriate that this last conversation be between Socrates and Plato. The two had never been comfortable with each other. Being so enamored as he was of the profundity of Socrates, Plato would often bumble forward in a way that was neither endearing nor amusing. He often would find himself being exquisitely inappropriate, out of place in word and deed, such that but a moment's forethought could have saved him the embarrassment but, alas, too late. Plato often played the social buffoon that would send him home in a depression that could be relieved only with the thought of the highest things disclosed by philosophy. Plato lived a loneliness that was exonerated only by the solitude of philosophical vision. Little could he have known that that solitude would become the foundation of a colossal cultural accomplishment that would be called the Western world. His appearance in Socrates' jail was neither expected nor unwelcome but simply an opportunity to exchange a few final words.

Socrates warmly greets his guest. "Plato, thank you for coming."

"My tears have dried so I thought I could risk a visit without descending into a blubbering idiot. It is so painful to think that Athens needs to kill you in order to feel better about itself. It's pure injustice."

Socrates responds. "Please don't be too harsh with your fellow citizens. In time of desperation there will be acts of equal desperation."

"But it's just so stupid."

"Respect the verdict just a little. There is a chain of causality that could end with a semblance of my guilt. It's a question of two theories of human nature. I'm seemingly guilty by one and perfectly innocent by the other. It's the difference between a material and a mental causality. As the reputed teacher of Alcibiades I did have some effect upon him and, in his promotion of the Sicilian disaster, it would follow that I bear some material responsibility. As the charges stated I may have taught him how to make the weaker argument stronger. All of this may be true if it is presumed that a strict material cause and effect is in play. A causes B which causes C., etc., with final disastrous results, I'm guilty. But, what is missing is the question as to whether there is instead a mental causality wherein one chooses for oneself what it is that one will do. There may be external and material influences but the final choice is one's own. With this view, I'm innocent. The problem is that a public jury, enflamed by passion and self-righteous outrage, cannot tell the difference and the theory of material causality will always win because it is seemingly more obvious. Of course with a jury the issue is not philosophical truth but finding someone to blame. Things could not be otherwise. It's the way of the world. Much the same could be said in another way. Recourse to all theories of material causality will find no one guilty, not even me, as it's just a series of material effects. The truth is though that there is only a mental causality or the freedom of thinking and doing for oneself, where each is responsible to himself for his own choice of deeds. Few have the courage of this, as one may call it a sort of transcendental reluctance, an unwillingness to see oneself in the nexus of the freedom of one's own choices. It is the laying in advance of an excuse or simply the sheer laziness of not shouldering the full weight of responsibility. As is often said, everybody wants an opinion, but nobody wants responsibility. Or, in another way, everybody may be entitled to his own opinion by democratic fiat, but no one is necessarily entitled to a true opinion. That, my friend, takes work. It's as difficult as the climb up Mount Parnassus. So, that is the way it is, people just being people."

Plato is crestfallen. "It's just doesn't seem right. It's to say that stupidity will always win. Is that the best we can do?"

Socrates is content. "Perhaps so, it is what it is. Alcibiades was a troubled soul. His father died too soon. At the age of 5 he is orphaned and the emotional devastation cut deeply but he learned to live with it. People felt sorry for him and early on he recognized that he would never be held accountable. His good looks simply exacerbated this and he was off to a lifetime of irresponsibility. Pericles tried to be a father figure but he was already a public father figure for the city and little could be left for the making of the small boy. In his youth he nurtured this resentment and loss and transformed it into the consummation of the dark side. An important distinction concerns the diverse nature of parental love, as the mother's is always unqualified and the father's qualified. The mother's is given freely, the father's is earned begrudgingly. Alcibiades never experienced the unqualified love of his mother or the qualified love of his famous father Cleinias who was just an image of the ghostly, in fact his illustrious ancestors were so replete with excellence that he could hardly measure up. Without a nurturing parental love, he found no footing in anything resembling a normal reality. The boy was haunted by an emotional absence and while he spent a life as a larger than life warrior, he finally was never much more than a little boy yearning for a childhood love that would never be. I entered his life almost as an affront. It was because of me that he took that dark side further into the abyss. He would prove me wrong, that all my talk of moderation and virtue was just a bunch of hooey reserved for those who were too weak to enforce the power of the negative. The whole world was his enemy, as a child devastated by an emotional loss would get even. He had the skills and the opportunity to take this vendetta very far, thousands died. That said, I did crack his façade, the example of my life gave him just enough pause to create a first glimpse of a conscience. He knew he wasn't perfectly evil and that it was just a game. That disturbed him further. The war gave him the largest stage for his criminality and run from conscience. I loved him dearly, just like everyone else, but I could finally do nothing for him, He chose for himself. My love is a great as my sadness. We shall now let him rest in peace. But perhaps one last thought. It was my privilege to have met two specially gifted boys, both having lost their parents, both equally desperate for Mommy and Daddy, and each alone finding neither. Their respective responses to their emotional losses set me to thinking early on about the limits of the conditions for the possibility of human choice. Each was instructive. The one chose the life of kindness and generosity as a shepherd upon a holy mountain and the other chose the life of deceit and cruelty that brought heartache to many in the city. In each case it had to be the freedom of choice and that alone that made the difference. Whatever our given circumstances, it is we ourselves who choose to be who we are. Excuses to the contrary may abound, but none hold up in the vortex of choice of "what am I to be?"

"Do you have any thoughts on how this war got started among us Greeks and how Athens came to be defeated? It just wasn't Alcibiades. What else can be said?"

Socrates takes a long distracted breath and replies. "Causes are much more hidden and further back in time than we usually expect. The final cause of our demise was the Will to Empire, or trying to-get-something-for-nothing. It is the policy of being-full-of-oneself and thinking that others will naturally concur. With the defeat of the Persians and the humiliation of Xerxes, we allied Greeks stood on the cusp of unimaginable prosperity. With the Persians rolled back to their rightful domain, we had the chance to choose peace and not war, we allies could cooperate through mutual respect and work together for the real benefit of all. We Athenians thought this but acted differently. The Delian League was formed under the rubric of high sentiment and mutual protection but it ended with central Athenian domination and a single minded self-interest that naturally spawned enemies. We never taxed ourselves. We thought that others ought to rightfully pay our way. Extracting that payment sent us down the road to war and our own demise, to the end of empire and, quite amusingly, my own execution. In becoming so full of ourselves we projected our empire further and further at a greater and greater cost. We naturally became entangled in the minding of the business of others, never just minding our own and that was the harbinger of our eventual doom. Costs then ballooned just to maintain our predominance, to be paid by those underfoot. Untenable situations will always reconstitute for the worse. In thinking we had the right to rule the world, we couldn't even rule ourselves. In projecting power outward we often found it directed back. In playing the bully, we invited many to be our enemies, perhaps still powerless but surely awaiting opportunity. The Spartans took the initiative and our arrogance and overextension signaled the end of empire. It took 27 years but end it would be. That, my friend, would be a brief summation." Plato has hung his head, listening intently, nearly in tears.

"How could we have done it differently?"

"A single word: retract. Get out of the racket of minding other people's business, pay our own way, and cooperate, not dictate."

Plato says dejectedly. "Is that possible?"

"The possible is whatever you choose it to be. Policies can be changed, long standing traditions circumvented, instances of injustice made good, it is our choice. The Will to Empire is like an addiction. It makes everything about one more and less. One is more narrow-minded, less respectful, more deceitful, less honest, more abusive, less generous, and finally more intent upon getting-something-for-nothing, and less aware of the damage that is done in the name of a high-falutin patriotism and self-absorption. To break an addiction steps are involved, distinct acts of the will that put one on the road to recovery and change from choosing the ever friendly negative to the ever more difficult positive. Guidance from the Idea of the Good is very helpful here. First of all, we must recognize the depth of our addiction and confront ourselves with neither hype nor pretense. We must see ourselves for what we are. But an even greater force lies beyond and is a power of infinite proportions. To this greatest power we must turn. Give up on being full of ourselves and defer to something far superior. To this comes the necessity to come clean, to acknowledge and then list the moral outrages that support the addiction. We must be perfectly explicit as to the wrongs committed. A separation then opens up between the monolith of imposing oneself unilaterally and the recognition that this is a complete and utter failure. With this insight one has already come to know oneself a bit better. The consequence here then is of course that the beauty of the unencumbered minding of one's own business erupts to illuminate the road to recovery. A life altering resolve is possible that is intent upon making the proper changes. It is no longer a game but a trial with one's life at stake. Positive action now becomes possible. List specific damages to specific parties and begin to make amends, restitution in the best faith possible. We Athenians could have collectively chosen this path of recovery. What is crucial is that any policy of retraction, of dismantling our attitude of empire that causes so much ill-will and harm, is akin to a personal recovery from addiction, and that one by one things can be done to further our recovery as a great city. Pulling out of areas where we don't belong would have been such a relief to those afflicted that they would have immediately become our best allies. Quit extracting and the pain goes away. Illustrative here is the theory of the big hole. Quit digging. A greater benefit is that we would have quit lying to ourselves, indulging in internal propaganda to make us feel better about doing the easy and the wrong things. Pay our own way. Getting-something-for-nothing is not cheap and sooner or later alien flagged warships will appear in our harbor seeking comeuppance. So, it was all very possible, breaking the addiction of empire and returning to a balanced and reasonable understanding of ourselves."

"If we were to look for another reason for our defeat in this war you may look to our attitude. We became a belligerent, pushy, bullying sort of people as we pushed the natural limits of the Delian League to the outer limits of our Athenian Empire. We began to believe in the ideology of competition. We came to compete with everyone in a game of winner takes all and with this we completely overlooked the much greater power of cooperation. When we came to believe that 'winning is the only thing' we were doomed. This forced us into a confrontational position in all of our dealings which accelerated our move to an overriding military position that cost more and more which we then passed on to those of our dominion. This vicious circularity contributed greatly to our decline as we invited everyone to hate us deeply for our presumptive arrogance. Had we thought more in terms of the benefits for all we may have done very much better. We gave people a legitimate reason to hate us when we could have inculcated the very opposite with mutual respect and consideration. The irony here is that we really don't believe in the superiority of this competition ourselves as instead most of us find the far greater personal satisfaction in precisely situations of cooperation. For example, the reason I cherish my army experience is the deep felt cooperation that is essential for any military success. It was each doing his special task in his contribution to the greater good of the group that was the most gratifying. We competed against the enemy surely, but we more significantly cooperated with each other in the fight against that enemy. Our unique democracy is similarly constituted. We compete vociferously in the Assembly over this or that but it is pure cooperation that allows for the possibility of the Assembly in the first place, as it is cooperation that forms the underlying consensus that ensures the differences of democratic government. Simply, with the romance of the ideology of competition one is always looking for a fight, a fight that you will get. It's a self-fulfilling prophecy that will be fulfilled, nothing wishy-washy about that. We began to pile up our losses. We got that fight in a total war to the finish, winner takes all, in which case it is all of our choosing. Imagine the difference had we just thought to cooperate instead?"

"Another matter of attitude or, perhaps just of presumption, compounded our attempts to run an Empire. We Athenians are rightfully special for having hit upon the political arrangement of democracy. It has served us incredibly well but at the same time equally poorly. Again an attitude made us stumble forward until we were flat on our face. We believed in the principle of personal and political freedom so much that we took it as an obvious universal, that is, that all peoples everywhere would desire an equal chance at democratic liberty. In our arrogance we became proselytizers. The belief in the universality of freedom is a fundamental error. Very slim indeed are the circumstances that create such a possibility. Our attempt to export democracy, to nation-build in our own image, is a mirage with dire consequences. Most peoples have a dictatorship or tyranny that they are perfectly comfortable with. The vast personal responsibility incumbent upon the democratic man has very little appeal to those already provided for in the rule of some few or some one. It is not personal freedom but rather security of power that most people find the most comforting. The personal ambitions of the marketplace of democratic culture will find few takers in most of the world. The Athenian mistake was to assume its enlightened political philosophy would fit all circumstances. It was simply incomprehensible when others said No. Caught up in the ideology of being the greatest city-state in the world, enamored of its own image of itself, productive beyond measure, Athens had absolutely no respect for the realities of others. That, of course, is an exquisite formula for disaster. Freedom is the exception, power is the rule, the universal, and presuming otherwise may be emotionally gratifying but it will prove to be the standard cause for further war and a perfect template for disaster, or the minding of other people's business."

Another aspect of our failure is that we assumed that it would be impossible for us to lose. Thinking ourselves superior in so many ways, victory was surely a given and with that we made it into a game, a sort of deadly sport. We knew there would be serious struggle and sacrifice but we thought ourselves to be finally invincible. That attitude allowed us to be talked into policies and strategies that were doomed, such as the invasion of Syracuse. We thought that such was but a plaything when in fact it led to our final defeat. We thought that surely all the gods were with us and we became like fools when faced with the utter facts of fighting for keeps. The Spartans never lost sight of the risks at stake and their strategy was a fight to the finish and that finally prevailed and we were defeated. Again, it is a common psychological malady, as we were full of ourselves to the maximum extent which set the terms for being as stupid as we could be and the slippery slope to our undoing became slicker and slicker.

"We need not be even now discouraged. As long as we are still alive something good remains to be possible and it is our rightful duty to do all that we can. It may not be probable but as long as it is possible we philosophers will stay the course. Remember

Plato that you have a perfectly unique responsibility. When one first understands the necessity of looking to the essential being of things, that invariant structure, all is changed for you personally. In the normal attitude, prior to this insight, one is encumbered of the multifaceted things of the world and accordingly is led to believe that the being of things is bound up in these matters of fact. Of course, how could one know anything different? It is the insight into essential being that sets up the distinction for the first time. It is from here that you will personally often look the fool, simply because this attitude involves a certain sense of dis-embodiedness. It is no longer the me of myself that recognizes this insight, but rather a sort of elevated ego that has been purified of all worldly content or, one could say, purified of psychological content. You may easily pass back and forth from this special ego to the me of myself as you so choose, but always appreciate the fact of the passage itself. The foolishness that people will naturally see in you is but your presence to this essential insight, to philosophical truth. They may judge you harshly but never be offended, it's the way of the world, they can't help themselves. It is not your place to become discouraged as it is nothing less than the highest privilege to have seen into essential being, something to which many have not the patience to achieve. It is a divine dispensation that will allow you to see an eternal grace in all things, a pantheism of the highest magnitude. Nothing could be more. Always cherish this inconceivable incommensurability."

Plato sits quietly for awhile, lost in a Socratic trance, as Socrates looks on with compassion for one so anguished. Here was a young man of philosophical tenacity that made him proud. He would carry forward a legacy that a judicial execution could not touch. The project of knowing thyself, the odyssey of the Western spirit, was in good hands.

Plato gathers himself. "With death so near, what concerns you?"

"The same things. Questions of immortality and virtue, matters of love and friendship, ideas of the Good and the Best. Same old, same old."

"But with time so short, what about yourself, what about your own death?"

"Plato, my friend, I couldn't be happier. It is the greatest opportunity of my life. Most people find death when they least expect it and when taken by surprise they can easily miss the moment. My execution by hemlock affords me the rarest of chances to pass over with my eyes open. As my extremities begin to numb I will be wide awake looking to see the sundry sights of illumination that will perfectly bedazzle. The immortality of the soul must require some such ecstasy and I want to experience that fully. If I can send back to you a message, I will. It's what I've been preparing for all my life. Ironically, the verdict of death isn't a punishment at all but deliverance and for that I thank the narrow mindedness of the jury. They know not what they do. Don't tell them. It will be our inside joke. Absolutely hilarious, don't you think?"

"Amazing, simply amazing," Plato smiles broadly.

"It's time for me to retire for the last time, big day tomorrow. I need to mull a few last things. Thanks again for coming as you are the most able to understand."

Plato rose and left without another word, saddened, exultant, and immensely unsure of the future.

☆ ☆ ☆ ☆ ☆

The morning broke bright and clear. The jailer Saul stalled as best he could but Socrates assured him that all was well and that events must go forward. The hemlock cocktail was served straight up with two Greek olives and a wine chaser. The prisoner looked oddly calm and took down the deadly potion in a single shot with a grin from ear to ear. He smacked his lips and laughed out loud, the oddest thing for our serious man of wisdom. There had not been much laughter in the past years in Athens. In due course he felt numb in the extremities and then dumb in the head and last of all he mumbled something about a chicken and a medicine man. The gadfly was dead, he was gone, off on his own to a place where others may more fully appreciate the depth and breadth of his great spirit. Thus was founded the condition for the possibility of the Western Spirit, something to which we are all beneficiaries and for which we must be eternally grateful.

☆ ☆ ☆ ☆ ☆

You the reader may have forgotten that it is I, the son of Thucydides, Thucydides the Younger, who has been speaking, narrating throughout. With the passing of Socrates my friendship with Plato deepened and while we were not the very best of friends, we shared that natural compassion that is common to people of the very same age. We were natural companions in time. I had lost my father to the war and Plato his mentor. We would meet occasionally and speak together on the nature of history. Plato would often bring his most promising student who would sit and attentively listen without saying much even though we encouraged him to contribute, his name was Aristotle. He was a bull of a human being, strong in ever way, with unbelievable strength and stamina. Had he wanted I'm sure he could have been an Olympic champion of some sort but his interests were more intellectual and scientific. Plato thought very highly of him and was certain he would carry on the project of philosophy in a vigorous and unique way. So the two of us talked about history and Aristotle listened. A single pair of questions refused any easy answer but remained central to our intentions. What is history? This was a seemingly easy enough general question but little could be done with it. We could get started but never went all that far. Our second question was more specific and was contingent upon an answer to the first and directly pertained to our own time. Does history repeat itself? In other words, could something like the fall of the mighty Athenian Empire happen again and, if so, what would be the inherent mechanism for such a recurring fall?

As I look at my hand I see and feel an appendage of myself that is simple enough yet when I consider, what may be called, the conditions for the possibility of that hand, there is nothing simple at all and considerations quickly get out of hand. That hand is mine as I am a result of my parents, their offspring, who have long since passed away and who in turn were similar products of their own parents and on again into a tradition of the past that is constituted of an indefinite series of generations. This legacy of the past is mirrored by a legacy into the future as my ancestors reflect my descendants as I sit looking at my hand. All that is given me is that existing hand yet these further horizons of time make up the conditions for my experiencing now. As a single individual one is already confronted with a vast series and network of possibilities and yet history is not about any single person but rather all persons in their mutual interactions across all of time, an edifice of colossal proportions. While our personal business is with the living that business is possible only as a miniscule point atop that gigantic flux that is the totality of the past, as this anticipates the future, an equally gigantic totality. Of course further questions from here are so vast that it is foolhardy to continue, save as a mystic, yet one stellar moment of convergence is possible. The network or nexus of all possible connections among persons now and throughout time seem to form an ideal structure of mental idealities that would be but another definition for the premise of the immortality of souls. To even be able to hint at any historical structure entails an underlying structure of ideal conditions. Knowing nothing more this must be the dimension of the immortality of the soul. Let's leave it at that. Neither Plato nor I could do much more at that point as we stood on the threshold of the simple mystery of being.

We felt infinitely fortunate to have gotten this far so we changed the subject. What about the fall of Athens? Our beloved city still retained some of the vibrancy of its more glorious past and the fact of no longer shouldering the burden of empire left it in a state of relative innovation and prosperity. At least we had not been exterminated like we had done to the Melians. But our immediate past loomed so largely that all of our surviving days would involve some thoughts about that shadow, we couldn't get away from it, perhaps happily so. I loved my father more and more as his memory faded into but a caricature of his real self. As he receded in my mind he became more like a god. I would have had it no other way, it was my most prized possession. Plato, too, deified Socrates as he went to work writing and writing some more. I never had much of a chance to read any of it but a few bits and pieces here and there that I did see indicated a man in search of the infinite. Plato's mental and spiritual concentration may have been the greatest achievement of our city and a city famous for achieving many other such superlative intellectual things. There is no way to know but Plato's writings may someday constitute the greatest collection of philosophical insight conceivable. This is not to say that it will necessarily offer any final answers but it will be the greatest possible beginning, a first impetus in an infinite task. As history moves forward Plato's writings form a legacy of eternal goodness and grace.

All of this aside, our second question regarding the repeatability of the Athenian fall is relatively straightforward. If people choose to do exactly the same thing there will be exactly the same results. Psychologically, it is in the nature of power as an experience of the individual or group that sets the spiral of repetition. Exercising power over another, choosing for them life or death, is an exquisitely divine experience. It is as if one were a god, or at least godly. Whether it is Alcibiades dictating, or the Athenian Assembly voting a decree, the decision on Melos to kill all the men, and sell all the women and children into slavery, is infinitely gratifying. I live, they die. I am the decider, I am like a god. This elixir of power is more gripping than any drug could be. Nothing in the moment could stand against this will to power or urge to annihilation, the dark side consummated. There will be no human responsibility, no one held accountable. For that single moment, one is god. The strength of this experience of power is the single greatest obstacle standing in the way of learning from the past. There can be no learning in the face of a man thinking he is a god and having the power to act unopposed. It is the ultimate instantiation of *hubris*, that arrogance which confuses the human with the divine and thinks itself perfectly other than it is. This arrogance will ensure the choice of power over against restraint every time. It is not that history repeats itself but rather it seems to recur simply because with each new generation of power brokers there is experienced that very same reality of divinity. In choosing to kill, I am no longer man but exist as if I were god. Of course nothing lasts, as proven by history. When removed from the pedestal of power the damage will be more readily seen and then the remorse sets in and the claim that this was all the work of a god and not me. Getting off the hook after the fact one must skedaddle and hide in the hills, or the suburbs of Dallas, if need be. Some few are caught and face the fact of their arrogance, standing before some sort of tribunal, The Hague for instance, and then they squirm and slither to maneuver in order to assert that the charges are false, all just fabrications of one's enemies, that the facts just ain't so. But everybody else will know better by now and the blame will be properly placed, perhaps. In his mind though it will always be someone else's fault even though he continues to long for the good old days when one could get away with murder in the name of the people and feel very good about it, indeed, exquisitely good. Tyrants of the world unite!

Such was the gist of our conversations. Plato and I, and the youngster Aristotle, quietly thinking through the difficulties of war and peace. Of course, we came to no final conclusions, just conversation, but at least for ourselves we felt that some progress may have been made, and that some honor had been bestowed upon the immortal souls of Thucydides the Historian and Socrates the Philosopher in the name of the Idea of the Good.

☆

Bibliography

Aeschylus, *The Oresteia*, translated by Ted Hughes, Farrar, Straus, and Giroux: New York, 1999.

Aristophanes, *Four Plays by Aristophanes: The Clouds, The Birds, Lysistrata, The Frogs,* translated by William Arrowsmith, Richmond Lattimore, and Douglass Parker, Meridan: New York, 1994.

Beard, Mary, *The Parthenon*, Harvard University Press: Cambridge, 2003.

Cartledge, Paul, *The Spartans: The World of the Warrior-Heroes of Ancient Greece: from Utopia to Crisis and Collapse*, The Overlook Press: New York, 2003.

Ellis, Walter, *Alcibiades*, Routledge: London, 1989.

Hanson, Victor Davis, *A War Like No Other: How the Athenians and Spartans Fought the Peloponnesian War*, Random House: New York, 2005.

Herodotus, *The Histories*, translated by Aubrey de Selincourt, revised with Introduction and Notes by John Marincola, Penguin Books: London, 2003.

Kagan, Donald, *The Peloponnesian War*, Viking Penguin: New York, 2003.

Kagan, Donald, *Pericles of Athens and the Birth of Democracy*, The Free Press: New York, 1991.

Meier, Christian, *Athens: A Portrait of the City in Its Golden Age*, translated by Robert and Rita Kimber, John Murray Publishers: London, 1999.

Meyer, Jack, *Alcibiades: A Play in Three Acts*, Trafford: Victoria, 2006.

Meyer, Jack, *The Odyssey of the Western Spirit: From Scarcity to Abundance*, Second Edition, Trafford: Victoria, 2007.

Plato, *The Collected Dialogues of Plato*, edited by Edith Hamilton and Huntington Cairns, Bollingen Series LXXI, Princeton University Press, 1961.

Plutarch, *The Lives of the Noble Grecians and Romans*, Volume I, Dryden translation, edited and revised by Arthur Hugh Clough, The Modern Library: New York, 1992.

Thucydides, *The Landmark Thucydides: A Comprehensive Guide to the Peloponnesian War*. Edited by Robert Strassler, Introduction by Victor Davis Hanson, The Free Press: New York, 1996.

Index

Aeschylus 55-58

Agathon 40

Aegospotami 129

Agis 108-110

Alcibiades 3, 6 (as a boy), 7, 15-17 (as a young man), 18-22 (Hipponicus), 22-23 (youthful outrages), 40-42 (symposium), 66-63 (Parmenides), 73-77 (Olympia), 77-82 (Melos), 100-101 (before Assembly regarding Sicily), 107-114 (Sparta), 114-131 (Persia), 126-127 (return to Athens), 130-131 (death)

Archidamus 29

Aristophanes 35-38, 58-60

Aspasia 7-13, 18, 27

Athens 4, 29

Aristotle 156

Bushwacker 90

Cave, Allegory of the 46-49

Clouds, The 58-60

Courage 96-97

Croesus 42-43

Decelea 110-111

Delian League 28, 98, 151

Delphi, Oracle at 42-55

Democracy 23-25, 142

Descartes 1

Diotima 7-13

Jack Meyer is an unaffiliated freelance
writer living in Wisconsin.

Contact at:
alcibiades399@gmail.com

·

www.ingramcontent.com/pod-product-compliance
Lightning Source LLC
Chambersburg PA
CBHW020509100426
42813CB00030B/3170/J